THE SC

THE SONG OF SONGS

*Selections from the sermons of
St Bernard of Clairvaux*

Edited by Halcyon Backhouse

HODDER AND STOUGHTON
LONDON SYDNEY AUCKLAND TORONTO

British Library Cataloguing in Publication Data
Bernard, of Clairvaux
   Sermones super cantica canticorum. The Song of songs
   1. Catholic Church. Sermons
   I. Title
   252.02

ISBN 0–340–53126–6

Contents

Editor's Note to 1990 edition

This new edition of Bernard of Clairvaux's famous sermons on the Song of Songs is published to coincide with the nine-hundredth anniversary of Bernard's birth. This edition is based on Dr S. Eales's translation, which was published by Elliot Stock in 1895. After his *The Twelve Steps of Humility and Pride*, and *On Loving God*, which Hodder and Stoughton published in 1985, Bernard's Song of Songs is his most well-known 'writing'. Bernard's original eighty-six sermons run to some six hundred pages, but only reach a quarter of the way through the Song of Songs. This present edition of the Song of Songs is a selection from these eighty-six sermons.

The introduction to Bernard, his life, background and his sermons on the Song of Songs in this edition are taken from Bruce Blaxland's introduction to the 1901 edition of the Song of Songs, which was published by Methuen. Wherever possible this introduction has been unedited and has only been updated in style where it was felt to be absolutely necessary. Again, Dr Eales's translation of the actual sermons has only been altered where the dictates of clarity have demanded this.

Halcyon Backhouse
Hampermill, 1989

INTRODUCTION TO
1901 EDITION

ST BERNARD'S LIFE

1 St Bernard's early life

It was in 1090, five years before Peter the Hermit preached the First Crusade through Western Europe that Bernard was born in the Castle of Fontaines in Burgundy. He was of noble birth. His father was a knight, Tescelin by name. He was able to live as a Christian knight, serving his temporal lord with head and hand, and at the same time rendering what he owed to the Lord his God. His mother was Alith, a daughter of Count Bernard of Montbar, and of the same family as the Dukes of Burgundy. At an early age she desired to follow the 'religious' life; but at fifteen she was married to Tescelin. They had six sons, of whom Bernard was the third, and one daughter.

As Alith was unable to follow what she considered the highest form of the Christian life, she did her best to come as near as possible to her ideal in the ordinary life of her home. She had not only performed with diligence the duties of mother and housewife in the castle, but she visited and often with her own hands tended the sick and poor in the neighbourhood. The fasts of the church were rigorously observed, and she tried to make the life in the castle – in all but name – the life of the convent. A holy man is said to have predicted that Bernard 'should guard the house of the Lord, like a faithful watchdog, that he should be a great preacher, and with his healing tongue should cure the wounds of many souls.' Whatever may be the truth about this prediction, we may trace the example of the parents in the life of the child: and say of them with truth, 'They were both righteous before God, walking in the commandments and ordinances of the Lord.'

We are not surprised to find that Alith's desire for her son was that he should adopt the life which she herself had so earnestly desired. She did not live to see her wish fulfilled as she died when Bernard was fourteen years old. But she may well have felt sure that he had a real vocation for the service of God when she saw in him seriousness and thoughtfulness beyond his years and a personal love for the divine Child, who according to his biographers, William and Alan, appeared to him on a Christmas Eve as the infant Saviour. 'And it is easy for those who have been wont to listen to his preaching to recognise with what abundance of blessing the Lord presented him on that happy night: for ever since he has seemed to possess a deeper knowledge in what relates to that divine Majesty, and a richer and more abundant flow of discourse respecting it.'

2 Bernard's conversion and early monastic life

It was some eight years after his mother's death, in 1113, that Bernard was 'converted'. He gave up, that is to say, his life to God and would henceforth live the life of the monk. His elder brothers were in the service of the Duke of Burgundy, and he himself might have followed their example. But after some period of indecision and severe mental struggle he decided to leave the world and to serve God. He was on his way to visit his brethren who were serving with the duke in his camp. He came to a church, dismounted, went within and prayed. The answer came and there was no more delay or indecision. Thenceforth Bernard was determined to obey the voice of God, who had plainly called him and 'to follow the Lamb whithersoever he goeth'. So in the spring of that year he gave up what appeared to be a life of worldly prosperity. Gibbon puts it

12

thus:

> In a secular life he would have shared the seventh part
> of a private inheritance; by a vow of poverty and
> penance by closing his eyes against the visible world, by
> the refusal of all ecclesiastical dignities [he refused the
> archbishoprics of Rheims and Genoa – the latter twice],
> the Abbot of Clairvaux became the oracle of Europe,
> and the founder of one hundred and sixty convents.

The historian states what is absolutely true with a sneer. Is
there not a suggestion of the motive of ambition? Would it
not be truer to history to suggest in Bernard's case that we
may here find an example of what Jesus was speaking
about when he said, 'no-one who has left home or wife or
brothers or parents or children for the sake of the kingdom of God will fail to receive many times as much in this
age and, in the age to come, eternal life' (Luke 18:29–30).

The decision was not only momentous for Bernard. It
was very important for the cause of the religious revival of
his day. Only seven years before his birth, Robert, a monk
of Molesmes, decided to withdraw from his monastery
and live a stricter life at Citeaux. In vain had he tried to
persuade his brethren to do this – and keep Benedict's
rule – at Molesmes. He with six others settled at Citeaux,
where the Duke of Burgundy granted them a site for their
building. There fourteen others soon joined him. These
men were the first Cistercians – an Order destined to
revive the religious life and to become a great power
through Western Europe.

The next year Robert was ordered by the Pope to return
to Molesmes. He obeyed and the house at Citeaux was
without a head. Alberic was chosen. The first code of rules
was drawn up during his life, and henceforth 'white' was
to be the colour which would distinguish the Cistercian
from the Benedictine. After ten years' rule Alberic died
and was succeeded by St Stephen Harding, an
Englishman. The first four years of his rule were years of

13

trial and anxiety. This was too strict for the majority of men – even if they desired to attain to perfection in the 'religious' life.

Their daily life would be as follows:

At two in the morning the great bell was rung and the monks arose and hastened from their dormitory, along the dark cloisters of the church. A single small lamp, suspended from the roof, gave a glimmering light, just sufficient to show them their way through the plain, unornamented building. After short private prayer they started Matins, which took them about two hours. The next service, Lauds, did not begin until the first glimmer of dawn was in the sky, and thus, in winter at least, a considerable interval occurred, during which the monk's time was his own. He went to the cloister and employed it in reading, writing, or meditation, according to his inclination. He then devoted himself to various religious exercises, until nine, when he went out to work in the fields. At two he dined; at nightfall assembled for Vespers, and at six or eight, according to the season, finished the day with Compline, and passed at once to the dormitory.[1]

It was into such a life that Bernard entered when he carried out his resolve. And it was just when the movement which Robert had begun seemed in danger of dying out that this resolve was taken. He would go to Citeaux. But he would not go alone. It is surely one of the greatest proofs of the sanctity and sincerity of Bernard that he was able to 'convert' his own relations. He went to his own house and family and told them 'what great things the Lord had done for him'. So with a party of thirty he set out for the Abbey of Citeaux. On the day after their arrival they were admitted to the novitiate.

So the stream turned. Men came and joined the Order from all quarters. New houses were formed: first, in the year when St Stephen received Bernard, Ferte, then Pontigny, the second daughter of Citeaux.

And then Clairvaux was founded, and Bernard himself was chosen to be its founder, in 1115.

Dean Milman says:

> There was a valley in Champagne, not far from the river Aube, called the Valley of Wormwood, infamous as a den of robbers: Bernard and his companions determined to change it into a temple of God. It was a savage, terrible solitude, so utterly barren that at first they were reduced to live on beech leaves: they suffered the direst extremity of famine, until the patient faith of Bernard was rewarded by supplies pouring in from reverential piety of the neighbouring peasants.[2]

It was during this struggle for existence that Bernard himself fell ill. He would have died if the common sense of his friend, the Bishop of Chalons, had not rescued him. He had ordained him, for he was now Abbot, and it was necessary that he should receive holy orders. It was during this time that he was able to begin the study of Holy Scripture and the Fathers, which enabled him to become the great preacher of his day. At this time too began that correspondence which in later days grew so much. It was now also at the suggestion of one of his biographers, William of St Thierry, that he began his Sermons on the Canticles.

3 Bernard's influence on the higher ecclesiastics

Bernard's influence, however, was soon to reach far beyond his own family, monastery and order. He began to do his best to reform the lives of the regular clergy. Cluny (with its enormous revenue and its Abbot, who could coin money, summon a chapter of 3,000 monks and relieve 17,000 poor in a year), an ex officio Cardinal, was the greatest religious house at the time. But Benedict's rule was not strictly observed, and Bernard was shocked at the luxury and laxity which prevailed. Even the splendid worship was in his eyes a weakness. For everything in the life of the true servant of God – the monk – in the church as well as elsewhere, should be as plain and simple as possible. During his own life the worship of the Cistercians and the adornment of their churches was as plain as the ritual of the service allowed. His attack on the Cluniacs was not forgotten. His relations with the Abbot of Cluny were never too friendly. Another great ecclesiastic received his rebukes in a different spirit. Suger – although an Abbot – was at the time practically Prime Minister of France. The Abbey of St Denis was closely connected with the Court. Bernard told him plainly what he heard – that soldiers, courtiers and women, entered the Abbey precincts. 'How could religious duties be attended to amidst such irregularity?' Suger listened to his words and obeyed.

But it was not only abbots or 'religious' people whom Bernard wished to reform. Archbishops and bishops were recalled to their duties. If his Apology to William the Abbot and his Epistles had had such an effect on the regular clergy – even on abbots like Suger – so his address to the Bishops of France was not without its effect also. Henry, Archbishop of Sens, returned to his diocese and gave up his worldly position. Stephen, Bishop of Paris, likewise left the Court, where he had been a great favourite with King Louis VI.

These things naturally brought the Abbot of Clairvaux prominently before the world. The last event brought him into conflict with the King and Pope. The story is similar to that of Henry II and Becket. The king resented the bishop's conversion. He seized his property. The bishop replied by putting his diocese under an interdict. At the same time he enlisted the sympathy of Bernard and the Cistercians. The appeal to Rome followed. And the Pope proved to be a broken reed for the bishop and his friends. In Bernard's letters we have the proof that 'he could stand before kings and not be ashamed'. He was not afraid to rebuke the Pontiff also. The king, however, at last made friends with Stephen and restored his property. He had lost his eldest son, which seems to have been the direct cause of the reconciliation; though from Bernard's letters to the Pope, he seems to suggest that the king would have yielded before had the Pope acted with more courage.

4 Bernard and the papal schism

The fame and influence of Bernard spread rapidly and widely; his irresistible preaching awed and won all hearts. Everywhere Bernard was called in as the great peacemaker in religious and even in civil dissensions. His justice, his mildness, were equally commanding and persuasive. It was a free and open court, to which all might appeal without cost; from which all retired, even if without success, without dissatisfaction; convinced, if condemned by Bernard, of their own wrongfulness.

He was the peacemaker in the greatest of all dissensions of his day. In 1130 Pope Honorius II died. There was a double election. Innocent II and Anacletus II were chosen. Who was to be the Pope? Who was the Anti-Pope? Bernard would decide. Soon after the election Innocent left Rome and landed in France. He asked King Louis to help him. The king summoned a council of prelates and nobles at Étampes. Bernard attended and was received as God's prophet. 'He opened his mouth and the Holy Spirit spake by it.'[3]

In a letter to the Archbishop of Tours, who hesitated to receive Innocent, he gave his reasons for his support. The best of the electors had chosen him – the majority had chosen him – Innocent led a better life than Peter Leonis. After this a supporter of the latter was either on the side of Antichrist or an Antichrist. England and Germany followed the example of France. Bernard became the constant companion of the Pope. He was also his constant adviser. Before his death, however, the Pope became estranged from Bernard. The schism lasted on through the life of Anacletus who died in 1138. Bernard had the satisfaction of receiving the pontifical insignia from his successor, Victor II.

5 Bernard in the south of France: his death

During the absence of the French king in the East, Bernard was busily opposing the heresies which had arisen in the centre and south of his dominions. Peter de Bruys had preached in Provence and Gascony at the beginning of the century. He attacked priesthood, sacraments and the worship of the church.

His place was taken by Henry – once a Cluniac monk. His influence was greater than that of Peter. The results are summed up in Bernard's Epistle 241: 'Churches are without people; people without priests, and in a word Christians are without Christ.' No sanctity was ascribed to the house of God – feast days were not kept – men died without penitence or Communion – and children were unbaptised.

First of all Alberic, the Bishop of Ostra, was sent for, as Papal Legate, to uproot the heresy. His mission was a failure. Then Bernard was sent for. The saint was received as an 'angel from heaven'. He preached constantly – explaining one by one the meaning of the Articles of the Faith. The result was quickly seen. At Albi where a mere handful of people had attended when the Legate celebrated Mass, the church was now thronged with worshippers. So he went about from town to town, from village to village. His love and fervour touched the hearts of the people. At last the heretical teachers fled from the places which he was to visit. When he had convinced his hearers he begged them to promise to listen no more to false teachers. After his return to Clairvaux he addressed a letter, Epistle 242, to the people of Toulouse beseeching them 'to stand fast in the Lord as ye have begun and as ye have heard of me'.

His life was now drawing to a close. He remained now,

as he had often wished, at his beloved Clairvaux. During his last years he was visited by the Prince of Portugal, the King of Sardinia, and for a second time by his friend, Malachi, Archbishop of Armagh. The last of these died soon after his arrival and Bernard wrote his life in 1148. Others whom he had influenced, such as Suger, were passing away from this world. Theobald, Count of Champagne – the friend and protector who had helped him to move his house at Clairvaux to a more healthy site – died in 1152. In May 1153 Bernard himself died. For some time he had been willing to depart and be with Christ. When his cousin, the Bishop of Langres, came to consult him about some Church affair he could not be moved to speak, though he had a short time before this taken a deep interest in this particular matter, as he had done in all matters connected with the Church. 'Marvel not,' he said, 'I am already no longer of this world.'

So the greatest ecclesiastic of his age passed away. We can learn from his writings what things he considered to be necessary for a true servant of God. Humility he looked upon as the greatest of virtues. 'To appear admirable to others and to think humbly of yourself this I judge to be the most marvellous among the virtues themselves' (Sermon on Canticles, 13:3). And, 'only those who are humble shall be rendered glorious with the wonderful and immortal splendour of that divine Lily' (Sermon on Canticles, 47:7).

And perseverance was the secret of all his success. He was never weary of doing good and was always ready to overcome evil with good. 'Strive therefore,' he says, 'for perseverance is the only virtue that receives the crown.'

To Suger on his 'conversion' he writes a long letter, and concludes with a curious but frequently used illustration about this virtue. He bids him 'join the head to the tail of the sacrifice'. The tail is the end of the body and a symbol of perseverance in, and the perfecting of, good works.

His words to the Genoese are well worth quoting as a good example of his correspondence. While writing about the papal schism, he takes the opportunity of speaking about his favourite subject.

And now what remains for me, dearly beloved, but to exhort you to perseverance, which alone wins for man glory, and for his virtues the crown of glory? Without perseverance the soldier does not obtain the victory nor the victor his crown. It lends vigour to the will and perfects all virtues, it is the nurse to merit, and the mediatrix between the battle and the prize. Perseverance is the sister of patience, the daughter of constancy, the friend of peace, the cementer of friendships, the bond of harmony and the bulwark of holiness. Take away perseverance and obedience loses its reward, doing good its grace and fortitude its praise. It is not he who has begun, but he that has preserved unto the end that shall be saved. When Saul was small in his own sight he was made king over Israel, but not persevering in humility, he lost both his kingdom and his life. If the caution of Samson and the devotion of Solomon had been persevered in, the one would not have been deprived of his strength nor the other of his wisdom. I exhort and beseech you to hold fast firmly to this gift of perseverance, the highest mark of honour, the one trusty guardian of integrity. Keep carefully what you have heard joyfully. Remember the words that are written of Herod: that he feared John and heard him gladly. Well would it have been for him, if he had been as ready to act as to listen. It is not they that hear merely who are called 'blessed', but they that 'hear the Word of God and keep it'.[4]

His fearlessness and single-mindedness are shown in his dealings with those in high authority. We have seen how he was not afraid to rebuke the Pope when he thought that he was not acting as worthy of his high position. This is not because he held any lower views of the prerogatives of the See of Rome than other saints or prelates of his age. His *De*

20

Consideratione contains many scathing rebukes; and he points out what he considered the blots in the government of the Church. It is also in the same work that we have the words addressed to the Pope: 'Consider before all things that the holy Roman Church, over which you preside by God's authority, is the mother, not the mistress of Churches; and that you are not the Master of the Bishops, but one of them.'

St Bernard was canonised in the pontificate of Alexander III, when he was enrolled among the 'Doctors' of the Church. Innocent III confirmed this title. He is also called 'mellifluous' in the 1508 edition of his works (Paris); and is generally recognised as the 'last of the Fathers'.

The following are the dates of some chief events of St Bernard's life:

1090	Birth of St Bernard
1113	His 'conversion'; he enters the monastery of Citeaux
1115	Foundation of Clairvaux
1130	Papal schism on death of Honorius II; Innocent II accepted chiefly through Bernard's influence
1135	He begins his exposition on the Song of Songs
1140	Peter Abelard condemned at the Council of Sens
1145	Eugenius III, his pupil, becomes Pope
1146	Eugenius commissions Bernard to preach the Second Crusade
1149	Return of the King of France, Emperor and other princes from the Crusade which ends in disaster
1153	Death of St Bernard at Clairvaux

ST BERNARD'S SERMONS ON
THE SONG OF SONGS

The sermons on the Canticles were intended to be an
exposition of this book in the holy Scriptures. There are
in reality sermons on the various subjects, which are
closely connected with the spiritual life of mankind. Bernard appears to have begun them in 1135. Mabillon, in
his preface, quotes the saint's biographer as follows:

> The man of God, having obtained an interval of quiet,
> occupied himself with other affairs; and, withdrawing
> into a bower formed of a trellis covered with sweet
> peas, he occupied himself in solitary meditations upon
> divine things. And suddenly there came to him in that
> divine hermitage, as to one sitting in the Lord's dwel-
> ling, songs of love, and feasts of spiritual nuptials. For
> a long time he poured forth his soul in meditation upon
> those things; he has expounded them in many forms;
> and it is manifest to all who read them how greatly he,
> who feasted daily upon these dainties, benefited
> thereby; and how great benefit we may also derive, for
> whom the remains of that blessing in the study of holy
> Scripture have been preserved.[5]

The second sermon shows us that they were begun in the
season of Advent. They were suggested by Bernard des
Portes, a Carthusian, to whom Bernard addressed two
letters on the subject (Epistles 153 and 154). 'I am sending
you the sermons on the beginning of the Song of Songs
which you asked for and I promised; and when you have
read them, I beg you to give me your advice as soon as
possible, whether I ought to give them up or proceed with
them.'

This appears to be the origin of the sermons as we have
them now. But Bernard's friend, William of St Thierry,

tells us that during the saint's enforced retirement through illness in 1117 he explained to him the Canticles. 'Every day for fear of forgetting what he had said to me, I wrote it down as well as God permitted me to do, and as my memory recalled the words.'[6] Mabillon refers to this as a briefer and different exposition.

St Bernard continued at intervals to preach the Canticles until the end of his life. He did not reach farther than chapter 3, verse 1. Bernard's constant attention to matters of Church and state, his visits to Rome and elsewhere, took him away from his monastery and made him, as he says, 'a monk only in his habit'. Hence, there were frequent interruptions in his sermons. But when at Clairvaux he appears to have preached daily. His reason for this was that as he could not perform the ordinary duties of labour imposed by the rule, he made up for it by study and preaching. 'It is a task not without some labour and fatigue for me to come daily to draw upon the streams, the open streams of Scripture, to give to each of you according to his need.' They were delivered at different times in the day, sometimes in the morning before Mass, sometimes in the evening.

In most manuscripts there are eighty-six sermons. The sermons on the Canticles, as we have observed, are not ordinary expositions of the book. There is no continuous interpretation of the text. However, Bernard always speaks of the Bridegroom as our Lord Jesus Christ and the bride is either the faithful soul or the Church. His interpretation therefore belongs to the Christian allegorical school.

The leading thought of the sermons is the presence of God in the soul of the creature of God. Man is being re-created after the 'image and likeness' of God. Hence the possibility of the close union between God and man, which is described in the Song of Songs under the illustration of the Bridegroom and the bride. Bernard could speak like this because he believed in the close presence of God to the soul. He disparaged all outward pomp and elaborate ritual in the church service in his desire to see that the Church was as plain and unadorned as possible. The material fabric was not the place where God could dwell. The souls of men and women are the most fitting shrine for the divine presence. So Bernard insists on the inward beauty of the bride. He does not care to think about the outer clothing of wrought gold.

It is the work of God the Holy Spirit within – the love of God – the humility which is the highest virtue and makes her most like the Bridegroom – the perseverance without which she will never attain to the blessed vision – these are the topics on which he never tires of preaching to the brethren. They are often also the subjects which appear in letters where we might least expect them.

In order to illustrate these things and other similar subjects Bernard quotes from all parts of holy Scripture, or uses phrases from Scripture. 'So studded are they everywhere with phrases drawn from the Old and New Testaments, as to form a jewelled mosaic, so skilfully and aptly introduced, that they might be thought to be suggested by the subject.' He had studied the ancient doctors of the Church. In his writings he quotes them very sparingly. Nearly every quotation and every Biblical allusion is from the Bible. Bernard used to say,

that he ascertained better the meaning of Holy Scripture, by drinking from the original fountain itself than from the streams running from it, i.e: the expositors of the text; yet he used to peruse pious and orthodox expositors, not with the idea of preferring his own opinion to theirs, but in order to form his own opinion upon theirs; and following faithfully the track made by them, he too used to quench his thirst at the fountain whence they had drunk before him.[7]

Bernard was always drawing with joy the water of life from these wells of salvation. His object was to attain to, and to lead others to attain to, the heavenly vision. His holiness and his devotion to this high object impressed itself deeply on the minds of men. It was through St Bernard, we do well to remember, that Dante attained the glimpse of the Beatific Vision.

Rev Bruce Blaxland MA, Vicar of Lilleshall, 1901

Notes

1 Usus Ord. Cisterc; in Morrison's Life, Bk 1, ch. 2
2 Hist. Lat. Christ, Bk. 8, ch. 4
3 Ernald, *Life of St Bernard*, ch. 1. 3
4 Epistle 129
5 Ernald, Book II, ch. 6
6 William of S. Thierry, *Life*, ch. 12, 59
7 Geoffrey, *Life*, Bk.1, ch. 24

SELECTIONS FROM THE
SERMONS ON
THE SONG OF SONGS

Sermon 1

On the title: 'Song of Songs'

It is necessary to speak to you, Christian friends, about different truths from those truths which people need to hear who are in the world, or at least we have to speak about these truths in a different way. To people who are in the world milk should be given and not meat, if a preacher wishes to follow the apostle Paul's method of teaching: 'I gave you milk, not solid food, for you were not yet ready for it' (1 Cor. 3:2). Paul himself teaches us, through his own example, to offer more solid nourishment to spiritual people, as when he says, 'This is what we speak, not in words taught us by human wisdom but in words taught by the Spirit, expressing spiritual truths in spiritual words' (1 Cor. 2:13). He also says, 'We . . . speak a message of wisdom among the mature' (1 Cor. 2:6). So be prepared to be nourished not with milk, but with bread. There is bread in these words of Solomon, from the Song of Songs, which is full of nourishment. We now place it before us and break it as we have need of it.

If I am not mistaken, you are sufficiently well instructed by the grace of God about the book of Ecclesiastes so that you can recognise and despise the vanity of the world which is spoken about in that book. And what about the book of Proverbs? Is not your life sufficiently ordered by the teaching of that book? Now that you have tasted both these loaves, which you have received as loaves from the chest of a friend, come close and taste this third loaf also, and see if it is not even better.

There are two principal evils, among others, which wage war against the soul. These evils are the vain love of the world and the excessive love of self. The two former books prescribe the remedy for each of these diseases, the former by cutting away, with the sharp knife of discipline, whatever is corrupt in the character and superfluous in the desires of the flesh: the latter, by wisely penetrating with the light of reason the deceitful glamour of this world's vanity and distinguishing it accurately from what is real and solid. Finally, Solomon prefers the fear of God and keeping his commandments to the pursuit of human knowledge and of worldly desires. 'Now all has been heard; here is the conclusion of the matter: Fear God and keep his commandments, for this is the whole duty of man' (Eccles. 12:13). This is absolutely correct. We have here both the beginning and the conclusion of true wisdom. For true and perfect wisdom consists in departing from evil and doing good. No one is able to depart completely from evil without the fear of God, just as no one is able to do good without keeping God's commandments.

Now that these two evils have been dealt with through the reading of Ecclesiastes and Proverbs it is possible to approach properly the fruit of these books as we listen to the sacred and sublime teaching of the Song of Songs. This teaching is only for the ears and hearts of those who have been disciplined and made wise. If the flesh has not been mastered by discipline and subjected to the Spirit, unless the burden of the glamour of the world has been despised and thrown away the heart remains impure and is not worthy to pursue the Sacred Song. Just as it is purposeless to shine pure light on blind eyes or closed eyes, so 'The man without the Spirit does not accept the things that come from the Spirit of God' (1 Cor. 2:14). For, 'the holy spirit of instruction flees deceitfulness, recoils from unintelligent thoughts, is thwarted by the onset of vice' (Wis. 1:5 NJB), that is, it runs away from people who lead undisciplined lives. Never will 'the Spirit of truth' (John 14:17) have anything to do with the vain things of this

30

world. What link can there be between the wisdom which is from above, and the wisdom of this world, which is foolishness in God's sight? 'For the wisdom of this world is foolishness in God's sight' (1 Cor. 3:19), and, 'the sinful mind is hostile to God (Rom. 8:7). But I think that the friend who comes to us on his journey will have no reason to murmur against us when he has eaten this third loaf.

But who is going to break this bread? The Master of the House is present, so you must recognise him in the breaking of the bread. Who else is capable of breaking the bread? As far as I am concerned, I am not rash enough to arrogate this to myself. If you are looking at me you will receive nothing. For I, too, am with those who wait to receive their meat from God. I beg God, with you, for the food of my soul and the sustenance of my spirit. Poor and needy as I am, I knock at the door of the One who opens and 'no-one can shut' (Rev. 3:7), so that I can receive a knowledge of the deep mystery which lies hidden in this book. 'The eyes of all look to you, and you give them their food at the proper time' (Ps. 145:15). Your little children seek bread and there is no one to break it for them. From your goodness we hope for that blessing. O most merciful One break your bread to the hungry souls who are before you, through my hands, if you see fit, through the power of your grace.

If you consult your own experience do you not know the victory that your faith has gained over the world? Do you not recall how you have come out of the abyss of misery and the filthy mire? Have you not also sung a new song to the Lord because he has done marvellous things? In the same way, when God set your feet on a rock and ordered your steps, in gratitude for the renewal of your life, a new song was put on your lips, a song of thanksgiving to God. After you had repented of your sin, God not only put away your offences, but has also promised you rewards. Has not that joy which inspired you with the hope of future blessings made you, 'sing of the ways of the Lord, for the glory of the Lord is great' (Ps. 138:5)?

31

Also, when someone finds light shining from a passage of Scripture that had previously been obscure and impenetrable, he will doubtless thank God for the nourishment he has received from the divine bread. Then he will go on to delight God's ear with the voice of joy and the sound of someone attending a feast. Finally there are the everyday struggles and battles which always face those who wish to live a godly life in Christ. The pressures may come from the flesh, the world or the devil, for a man's earthly life is one long struggle. As you experience this all the time, you must, every day, sing new songs of thanksgiving to God for the victories which you gain.

As often as temptation is overcome, ungodly desires restrained, imminent danger avoided, a trap of the tempter discovered or some longstanding fault finally overcome, you are to praise God. Whenever some special favour you have been seeking for many years is granted by God you should follow the prophet's example and express your thanksgiving to God for all his gifts, with 'thanksgiving and the sound of singing' (Isa. 51:3). Anybody who is not able to sing to God, 'Your decrees are the theme of my song wherever I lodge' (Ps. 119:54), will be found full of ingratitude on the day of judgment. As you make progress in your spiritual life so you ought to sing to God's praise and glory, for he has inspired every spiritual step you take. I do not see how else the following verse can be true: 'Shouts of joy and victory resound in the tents of the righteous' (Ps. 118:15). How else can the beautiful and salutary exhortation of the apostle become a reality: 'Speak to one another with psalms, hymns and spiritual songs. Sing and make music in your heart to the Lord' (Eph. 5:19).

There remains, however, a Canticle which because of its excellence and incomparable sweetness rightly surpasses all those I have mentioned, as well as any I have not mentioned. This Canticle I call the 'Song of Songs', since it is the fruit of all the others. Only the anointing of God's grace teaches us this Canticle and only through experience does the soul come to know it. People who have experienced it know it well. Those who have not enjoyed this happiness must earnestly seek it, so that they do not just have a factual knowledge about it, but so that they experience it for themselves in their souls. It is not a cry from the lips, it is joy in the heart; it is not a noise coming from the mouth, but the welling of inner joy; it is not a string of words it is the harmonious movement of the will. It is not heard by anybody else. Only she who sings and he in whose honour it is sung, that is the Bridegroom and the bride, hear the strains of the song.

It is a nuptial song, which is expressive of the chaste and sweet emotions of souls, the entire conformity of character, the blending of affections in mutual charity.

Sermon 3

What it is to kiss the Lord's feet, hands and lips

'Let him kiss me with the kisses of his mouth' (S. of S. 1:2).
We shall read today from the book of experience. Turn
your minds in on yourselves and let each of you examine
your own conscience about the things which will be mentioned. I wish to find out if any of you feel compelled to
speak out of the deep desire of your heart about the
words of the text which we are about to consider. Not
everyone can sincerely take these words on their lips, but
only those who have received the spiritual kiss from the
lips of Christ. Such people constantly seek to be renewed
with what they have found to be full of such sweetness. I
feel certain that nobody can understand what this is
unless they have experienced it for themselves. It is like
the hidden manna which when it is tasted still leaves the
person hungering for more. It is a fountain that strangers
cannot draw from because they cannot see it, and yet
those who do drink from it desire to drink from it again
and again. Listen to the words of someone who has
experienced what he has sought: 'Restore to me the joy of
your salvation' (Ps. 51:12). No soul, such as mine, which is
laden with sin, subject to the desires of the flesh, which
has not tasted the delights of the Holy Spirit and which is
completely ignorant of, and inexperienced in, inner joys,
can even pretend to have achieved such a degree of grace.

Nevertheless, I shall point out to such a person the saving grace which is appropriate for him. He must not be so

rash as to lift himself up to the lips of the divine Bride-groom. Rather, let him lie in holy reverence at the feet of the Lord, who is also our judge. Let him be like the tax collector in Jesus's parable, (see Luke 18:9–14), who trembled before God and would not even lift up his eyes to heaven in case his eyes, which were so used to earthly darkness, should be dazzled by the light of heaven and be blinded by its glory. The tax collector would have been overcome by the splendour of God's majesty and over-whelmed again in an even greater darkness.

It is not right for you, sinful soul, whoever you are, to look at the place and the posture of the woman men-tioned in Luke 7:37, who had been a sinner and who became a saint. She had thrown off her sins and put on holy clothes, since she had been vile and contemptible. This is the place where the Ethiopian changed her skin and was restored to a new whiteness, and was enabled to respond with as much confidence as truth to those who reproached her: 'Dark am I, yet lovely, O daughters of Jerusalem' (S. of S. 1:5).

If you wonder how she was enabled to do this, or by what means she obtained it, I will give you a brief reply. She wept bitterly, she drew long sighs of remorse from her soul, her body was convulsed with salutary sobs and in this way the deeply embedded poison was rooted out. The heavenly Doctor came quickly to her aid: for 'his word runs swiftly' (Ps. 147:15). Is not the word of God a medicine? It is indeed a strong and powerful medicine which 'searches minds and hearts' (Ps. 7:9). 'For the word of God is living and active. Sharper than any double-edged sword, it penetrates even to dividing soul and spirit, joints and marrow; it judges the thoughts and attitudes of the heart' (Heb. 4:12). Follow the example of this penitent, unhappy soul, and prostrate yourself so that you may stop being unhappy. Prostrate yourself down to the ground, embrace our Lord's feet, appease them with kisses, cover them with your tears. You do this, not in order to wash his feet, but in order to cleanse yourself; you do this so that you may become like one of the sheep 'just shorn, coming up from the washing' (S. of S. 4:2). And do not be presumptuous and lift up your eyes, which are flooded with tears of shame and grief, until you also hear the words of absolution, 'Your sins are forgiven' (Luke 7:48), and until you hear God say, 'Shake off your dust; rise up, sit enthroned, O Jerusalem' (Isa. 52:2).

Once you have placed this first kiss on Christ's feet you must not assume that you can immediately stand up and kiss his lips. You must kiss his hand and see this as a way of making progress, and a second step, by which you reach a greater blessing. Understand the reason for this. If Jesus had said to me, 'Your sins are forgiven', and I did not stop sinning, what benefit would it be to me? What is the point of my taking off my clothes if I then put them on again? Or, if I wash my feet and then make them dirty again will I benefit at all from having washed them?

I have lain down for a long time in the dirty mire, wallowing in every kind of vice. If I do escape from this but then later on fall back into the mire my subsequent state will doubtless be worse than my original condition. I remember how the One who healed me spoke to me, 'See, you are well again. Stop sinning or something worse may happen to you' (John 5:14). The One who gave me the will to repent from the past needs to give me grace so that I may abstain from sin in the future. Then I will not go on sinning and make my last state worse than my first state. Woe is me if the One without whom I can do nothing should suddenly take away his supporting hand from me, just as I am being penitent!

I repeat, I am capable of doing nothing without him. I am not able to repent of the past or keep myself from new sin. I keep in mind the counsel which the wise man gives: '. . . do not repeat yourself at your prayers' (Ecclus. 7:14 NJB). I tremble at the sentence which the Judge had in his mind when he pronounced, 'The axe is already at the root of the trees, and every tree that does not produce good fruit will be cut down and thrown into the fire'

(Matt. 3:10). I confess that I shall not be completely satisfied with the former grace which has enabled me to repent of my previous sins. I shall not be content until I have received God's second gift of grace which enables me to bear fruit which is worthy of penitence and prevents me from returning to my former pollution.

I must ask and receive this before I presume to approach the higher and more sacred degrees of blessing. I do not wish to arrive at the highest point suddenly but to make progress towards it gradually. Just as the shamelessness of a sinner is displeasing to God, so, in the same way, the humility of a sinner is pleasing to him. The more you take note of the increase in your desire for God and the more you do not seek greater spiritual privileges for yourself, the more you will please God.

There is a great distance between and a long climb up from the feet to the lips and it would be a great lack of reverence to go from the feet straight to the lips. Do you think that you, who are still stained with marks of recent sins, can touch those sacred lips already? You were only drawn out of the mire yesterday and so cannot aspire today to the glory of Christ's face. You must pass through an intermediate stage which is Christ's hands. These will first of all cleanse you from your sin and then lift you up. But how shall Christ's hands lift you up? By giving you the basis for aspiring to the higher life which consists in God's grace of self-control, fruits which are worthy of penitence and pious deeds. These gifts will lift you up from the manure heap and infuse in you the hope of higher things. As you receive these gifts you will certainly kiss the hand of the Lord, as you give glory to him and not to yourself. You must give him glory not once, but twice. The first time you give him glory you do so because he has forgiven your sins, and the second time because of the virtues which he has given you. If you do not do this how would you reply to the following reproaches? 'What do you have that you did not receive? And if you did receive it, why do you boast as though you did not?' (1 Cor. 4:7).

Once you have double proof through these two kisses of God's breathtaking humility you may then be bold enough to try to move on to higher and more sacred things. As you grow in God's grace, so your confidence will increase and your love will grow in fervour. Then you will be enabled to ask, seek and knock, knowing that it will be given you, you will find and the door will be opened to you (see Matt. 7:7). When you are in this state of mind and soul I believe that you will not be refused the highest and most sacred kiss of all which encompasses both supreme condescension and unutterable sweetness.

This is the way and the order that must be followed. First, we fall at the feet of the Lord our Creator and lament our sins and faults. Second, we seek his helping hand to lift us up and to strengthen our feeble knees so that we may stand upright. Third, after we have with many prayers and tears received these two graces we may perhaps dare to lift up our eyes and view the Lord's glorious and majestic face. We are not only to adore him, but we are (and I say this with fear and trembling) to kiss him, because the Spirit in front of us is Christ the Lord, to whom, being united in a holy kiss, we are by his marvellous condescension made to be one Spirit in him.

It is indeed only right, Lord Jesus, that my heart has declared, 'Your face, Lord, I will seek' (Ps. 27:8). You have enabled me to hear your mercy in the morning as I lay prostrate in the dust kissing your sacred imprints. You have forgiven the evil of my previous life. Then, as the day of my life continues, you have made the soul of your servant joyful through kissing your hand when you have given me grace to carry on living well. Now, what is left, good Lord, if you do not let me come into the fullness of your light as I kiss your divine lips, in my fervent spirit, and am filled with your joyful presence? Teach me, most dear and peaceful One, teach me where you live and where you rest at noon.

Sermon 6

How mercy and judgment are the feet of God

I must not forget to refer to those spiritual feet of God which it is necessary for the penitent, first of all, in a spiritual and mystical sense to kiss. I know the state of your enquiring minds which refuse to pass over the smallest detail without a full examination. It is important to know what is meant by the phrase 'the feet of God' which occurs so frequently in Scripture. Sometimes God is depicted as standing, 'We will worship in the place where his feet have stood' (Ps. 132:7 Vulgate); sometimes as walking, 'I will walk among you and be your God' (Lev. 26:12); and sometimes as running, 'like a champion rejoicing to run his course' (Ps. 19:5). If the apostle Paul felt that it was right to speak about the head of Christ as the Deity, 'the head of Christ is God' (1 Cor. 11:3), then I think that we may properly speak of his feet as being Christ's humanity, and call them 'mercy' and 'judgment'. Judgment and mercy are two words which are familiar to you, and if you reflect, there are many passages in the Scriptures where these words are so used. God took the foot of mercy when he became man and this is taught in the book of Hebrews, 'For we do not have a high priest who is unable to sympathise with our weaknesses, but we have one who has been tempted in every way, just as we are – yet was without sin' (Heb. 4:15). It can be seen that it is appropriate to call Christ 'the foot of judgment from the following verse, 'And he has given Christ authority to

39

judge because he is the Son of Man' (John 5:27).

These two feet exist under the divine head and as such a woman gave birth to the invisible Emmanuel, under the law and was seen on earth talking with men. On these two feet Christ comes to us now, but spiritually and invisibly, benefiting and healing those who are oppressed with the devil. On these feet Christ comes to the souls who are dedicated to his service, enlightening and constantly penetrating the hearts and souls of the faithful.

Happy is the soul on which the Lord Jesus has placed his feet! There are two signs by which you can recognise these souls which will be imprinted by divine footsteps. These two signs are fear and hope. Fear is the imprint of judgment and hope is the imprint of mercy. That is why it is said, 'The Lord taketh pleasure in them that fear him, in those that hope in his mercy' (Ps. 147:11, AV). 'The fear of the Lord is the beginning of knowledge' (Prov. 1:7, AV), hope continues this hope in the soul and love is the culmination and completion of wisdom.

Because this is the case great benefit is derived from the first kiss which is given to the feet of Christ, so long as neither of the feet is left out. If you mourn deeply over your sins and fear God's judgments then you will have pressed your lips on the footsteps of truth and judgment. If you moderate that fear and mourning for sin with the thought of God's goodness and with the hope of obtaining pardon then you will know that you are embracing the foot of mercy.

It is not, however, expedient to embrace the one without the other. If you think about judgment in isolation the soul is plunged into an abyss of despair. If you reflect on mercy exclusively it may lull you into a false sense of security and just deceive your own mind.

I have been privileged as a miserable sinner sometimes to sit at the feet of the Lord Jesus and to embrace one foot and then the other with as complete a devotion as his loving kindness has enabled me to feel. But if I was ever pricked by my conscience I forgot about mercy and

40

became absorbed with the thought of judgment. Then I was quickly oppressed by incredible fear and shame, surrounded by the darkness of horror, so that I could only tremble and cry out, 'Who knows the power of your anger? For your wrath is as great as the fear that is due to you' (Ps. 90:11). If, however, I moved on from the foot of judgment to the foot of mercy too quickly I became negligent and indifferent to my own sin. Then I quickly became less earnest in prayer, less quick to act, more inconsiderate in my speech and more prone to idle laughter. I became less steady and stable in all my character, both inwardly and outwardly. Now that I have learned from the best of all teachers, experience, I no longer rely on judgment alone or on mercy alone, but 'I will sing of your love and justice' (Ps. 101:1). I will never forget these two sources of judgment, for they will always equally be my songs in the house of my pilgrimage. Until mercy is exalted high about judgment my unhappy condition shall remain. Only then will the glory that has been given to me inspire my hymns of praise to you, Lord God, when pain and grief will be totally absent for ever.

Sermon 8

God's kiss is the Holy Spirit; the Church asks for this kiss so that she may know the Holy Trinity

It seems to me that as Christ said, 'No-one knows the Son except the Father, and no-one knows the Father except the Son and those to whom the Son chooses to reveal him' (Matt. 11:27), he has decreed that there should be a particular unutterable kiss which is unknown to any created being. For the Father loves the Son and embraces him with a love that is unlike any other. Here the supreme God is embracing his equal and the eternal his co-eternal. God the Father is united to the Son by no less an affection than that which comes from the Son, as he attests when he says, 'but the world must learn that I love the Father and that I do exactly what my Father has commanded me. Come now; let us leave' (John 14:31). Here Christ is doubtless referring to his Passion. What other than a deeply mysterious and sweet kiss can be the recognition of mutual love between the One who is created and the Creator?

I am certain that even angels do not experience the secret of this divine love which is both so august and so sacred. St Paul knew this when he spoke about a peace that passes the understanding of even the angels. This is why even the bride is not bold enough to ask for this as it is reserved for the Father alone. The bride's request is a lesser one.

Notice that the new bride receives fresh proof of the

affection of her Bridegroom, but this is not the kiss mentioned above. Speaking about Jesus breathing on his apostles, that is the early Church, St John says, 'he breathed on them and said, "Receive the Holy Spirit."' (John 20:22–3). Undoubtedly it was a kiss that he gave them. Was it in the physical breath? No. It was the invisible Spirit who communicated through the Lord's breathing, so that everyone would understand from this action that the Spirit comes equally from the Father and the Son. It is enough for the bride to receive the gift of grace from her Bridegroom, although this is not the highest grace of all. But nobody should think that this is a small favour and of little value, for it signifies nothing less than the reception of the outpouring of the Holy Spirit. If it is right to understand that it is the Father who gives the kiss and that it is the Son who receives the kiss we shall be correct in thinking that the Holy Spirit is the kiss. For the Holy Spirit is the constant peace, the indivisible love, the unbreakable unity between the Father and the Son.

It is therefore by the power of the Holy Spirit that the bride has the boldness to ask in faith using this same name that she may receive the outpouring of the Holy Spirit. She holds a pledge, as it were, so there is no shadow of presumption in her request. I am talking about the declaration of the Son when he said, 'No-one knows the Son except the Father, and no-one knows the Father except the Son and those to whom the Son chooses to reveal him' (Matt. 11:27).

The bride has no doubt that if God wishes to grant this knowledge to anybody it will be to her. Therefore she prays boldly that this may be given to her, in whom both the Father and the Son is revealed. For the Father is not revealed without the Son and the Son is not revealed without the Father. This is in line with the saying, 'Anyone who has seen me has seen the Father' (John 14:9). 'No-one who denies the Son has the Father; whoever acknowledges the Son has the Father also' (1 John 2:23). From these verses it is clear that the Son is not known

43

without the Father, and the Father is not known without the Son. Jesus also said, 'Now this is eternal life: that they may know you, the only true God, and Jesus Christ, whom you have sent' (John 17:3). From this it follows that Jesus attached the highest importance to knowing both the Son and Father. Finally, we read that those who follow the Lamb have his name and the name of his Father written on their foreheads (see Rev. 14:1 RSV). This means that their knowledge of each divine person is a glorious experience for them.

You, brethren, must behave prudently as you search for the divine mysteries. You must bear in mind the warning of the wise man, 'Do not try to understand things that are too difficult for you, or try to discover what is beyond your powers' (Ecclus. 3:21 NJB). Walk with those exalted subjects in the Spirit and do not live according to your own judgments. The teaching of the Spirit does not increase curiosity, but it does increase charity. When the bride is seeking the person her soul loves she is correct neither to trust the judgment of human passion nor to follow the futile thoughts of human curiosity. Rather, she prays for the gift of the Holy Spirit: she invokes the Holy Spirit so that through him she may receive both the love of knowledge and also the necessary grace to go with it. It has been well said that the knowledge that is given in this way comes with a kiss since a kiss is a sign of love. But the kind of knowledge which 'puffs up' (1 Cor. 8:1) and which is devoid of love is not given. Those who are 'zealous for God', but do not have a zeal that is 'based on knowledge' (Rom. 10:2) do not arrogate this to themselves at all. But the Holy Spirit's gift of knowledge gives both the light of knowledge and the blessing of piety. For the Holy Spirit is the Spirit of Wisdom and the Spirit of Knowledge. Just as the bee produces honey and wax so the Holy Spirit kindles the light of knowledge and infuses God's grace in the soul.

Anyone who has knowledge without love, or love without knowledge has not received the Holy Spirit's gift of knowledge, since this gift has no place for error or lukewarmness. This is why the bride, who wishes to receive this double gift, offers both her lips. In this way her reason is full of intelligence, and her will is full of love for heavenly wisdom. She experiences complete joy, receives the perfect divine embrace and is delighted to hear the words, 'your lips have been anointed with grace, since God has blessed you for ever' (Ps. 45:2).

When the Father kisses the Son, the Father gives the depths of his complete divinity and also breathes on the Son the sweetness of his love. The Scripture intimates this when it says, 'Day after day they pour forth speech' (Ps. 19:2). No created being can experience this eternal, unique and blessed embrace. Only the Spirit, who is both with the Father and with the Son, is aware of and a witness to that mutual recognition and love. As the apostle Paul wrote, 'Who has known the mind of the Lord? Or who has been his counsellor?' (Rom. 11:34).

However, someone might reply, 'How can they come to a knowledge of what you say is hidden from the understanding of all creatures?' For, 'No-one has ever seen God, but God the One and Only, who is at the Father's side, has made him known' (John 1:18). Yes, it is God the Father who reveals God the Son. But he does not reveal him to a sinful man like me, who is so totally unworthy of such an honour, but to the friend of the Bridegroom, John the Evangelist, the disciple whom Jesus loved. Because John's soul pleased God he is worthy of being called the disciple whom Jesus loved, and he is worthy to receive the dowry of the bride, the embraces of the Bridegroom and then worthy to sit next to Jesus at the Last Supper. But he was not the only person who was to receive this great divine gift. This gift is for all who hear the words, 'I have called you friends, for everything that I learned from my Father I have made known to you' (John 15:15).

The apostle Paul also knew about this, as we see when he wrote, 'I want you to know, brothers, that the gospel

I preached is not something that man made up. I did not receive it from any man, nor was I taught it; rather, I received it by revelation from Jesus Christ' (Gal. 1:11–12).

Undoubtedly, all these holy men can with truth and happiness say to us, 'No-one has ever seen God, but God the One and Only, who is at the Father's side, has made him known' (John 1:18). This revelation was none other than the giving of this sacred and eternal embrace, as it is said, 'I and the Father are one' (John 10:30), and 'the Father is in me, and I in the Father' (John 10:38). This is indeed, as it were, a kiss, but one which no creature can approach. It is a loving and peaceful kiss, but the love transcends all knowledge and the peace transcends all understanding. '"No eye has seen, no ear has heard, no mind has conceived what God has prepared for those who love him" – but God has revealed it to us by his Spirit' (1 Cor.2:9-10), that is with a kiss from his mouth. So the relationship of the Father with the Son, and the Son with the Father, is, so to speak, a kiss from the mouth. We read where this comes from and what it consists of in the following words, 'We have not received the spirit of the world but the Spirit who is from God, that we may understand what God has freely given us' (1 Cor. 2:12).

We must make a clearer distinction between these two. The person who receives the fullness of God himself has received the complete gift, while the person who has only received the benefits of God's fullness. The apostle Paul was indeed a great man, but no matter how high God raised him up and even though he was elevated to the third heaven, he still remains far below the face of the most high God. Paul had to resign himself to living within the confines of his own human condition. Since Paul is unable to face God's glory he has to plead with God so that God will come down to him in his mercy and send him a gift from on high. But he 'Who, being in the very nature God' and, 'did not consider

46

equality with God something to be grasped' (Phil. 2:6), could say in complete confidence, 'I and the Father are one' (John 10:30). Jesus Christ could do this because he is united to the Father as an equal and because he is embraced by him as an equal. He is not in the position of having to beg for the gift as if he were in some way inferior. Jesus is linked in an embrace with the Father because they are of equal rank. Jesus receives a privilege which is his by right, and is only for him. So, for Christ, the kiss from the Father is when he experiences the fullness of God, but for Paul it is only a participation of divine love.

Nevertheless, anyone who receives this sign is happy because through it comes both the knowledge of God and the love of God, our Father. For God cannot be completely known if he is not at the same time completely loved. Who among you has ever experienced in the depths of his conscience the spirit of the Son crying, '*Abba*, Father' (Gal. 4:6)? That soul which feels itself animated by the same spirit as the Son, that soul, I say, may believe that it is the object of the affection of the Father. Soul, no matter who you are, trust in God the Father that you are in such a happy state. Trust in God and do not have any doubts. In the spirit of the Son recognise that you are a daughter of the Father, the sister or the bride of the Son. The proof for this is close to hand and it will not be difficult to produce. For what does the voice of the Bridegroom say to her? Does she not say, 'I have come into my garden, my sister, my bride' (S. of S. 5:1)? She is your sister because she has the same Father as you; she is your wife because she has the same Spirit of God in her as you have. If a human marriage enables two humans to become one flesh, will not a spiritual union make an even greater bond in the Spirit? In fact the apostle Paul declares, 'he who unites himself with the Lord is one with him in spirit' (1 Cor. 6:17). Also listen to how lovingly and humbly God names her as his daughter. As his daughter-in-law God the Father invites her to the kind embrace of his Son, 'Listen, O daughter, consider and give ear: Forget your people and your father's house. The king is enthralled by your beauty; honour him, for he is your lord' (Ps. 45:10-11). It is from him that she makes her request. But, holy soul, stay in the deepest reverence, for he is the Lord your God. He is not to be embraced when it suits you, but rather, he is to be adored with the Father and the Holy Spirit for ever and ever, Amen.

Sermon 13

The duty of praising God for his good gifts

As the sea is the source of fountains and rivers so the Lord Jesus Christ is the source of every kind of virtue and knowledge. For who but the King of Glory is the Lord of every virtue? According to the song of Hannah he is the Lord God of knowledge (see 1 Sam. 2:3). Self-control of the body, diligence in the heart and correct judgment from the will flow from a divine source. And that is not all. For anyone who has a keen intellect, or who is a powerful orator or has a saintly character also has his ability given to him by God. Every wise conversation that is full of knowledge has its origin in God, 'in whom are hidden all the treasures of wisdom and knowledge' (Col. 2:3). Do not pure intentions, just judgments, holy aspirations all stream from that same source? All waters constantly seek to return to the sea. They sometimes make their way there through hidden and underground tunnels so that they can continue their journey and they become visible again and useful to man. So why are those spiritual streams not constantly and wholeheartedly attributed to their legitimate source and allowed to continue to flow in the fields of our hearts?

Let the rivers of varying graces return to their source so that they may flow again. Let the heavenly rains rise again to their heavenly source so that they may be poured out again and even more abundantly on the earth. Do you ask, How does this happen? In the way that is laid down by the apostle Paul, 'give thanks in all circumstances' (1 Thess. 5:18). Whatever you may think that you have by way of wisdom and virtue, attribute it to the One who is the Power of God and the Wisdom of God, that is, to Christ.

Not every offering of thanks is acceptable to God, but only those which come from a sincere and pure heart. I say that these offerings must come from a pure heart because some people boast about their bad actions, and even give thanks to God for them. Let anyone who does this listen to these terrifying words, 'You speak continually against your brother and slander your own mother's son. These things you have done and I kept silent; you thought I was altogether like you. But I will rebuke and accuse you to your face' (Ps. 50:20–1). I also say that these people must be sincere because of the hypocrites who do indeed glorify God for their good deeds, but do so only with their lips. In their hearts they reserve all praise for themselves and because they behave so deceitfully in God's presence their sin is detestable.

The first group of people, in their sin, attribute to God their own bad actions, while the second group of people deceitfully arrogate to themselves the good things which they have received from God.

As far as the first group of offences is concerned, they are so full of worldliness and stupidity, and are, in a sense, so obviously wrong, that it is hardly necessary for me to warn you against them. But the second group contains the most prevalent besetting temptation among religious and spiritually minded people. It is undoubtedly a great, a very rare virtue to be able to perform great deeds without having a sense of one's own greatness. But a person's holiness should be hidden from himself although it may be apparent to other people. I consider that being admired by others while remaining really humble is the most marvellous of all virtues. You are truly a faithful servant if you just remain humble with yourself when the glory of the Lord comes from you or passes through you.

Then you will be doing what the prophet Isaiah wrote about, 'He who walks righteously and speaks what is right, who rejects gain from extortion and keeps his hand from accepting bribes, who stops his ears against plots of murder and shuts his eyes against contemplating evil – this is the man who will dwell on the heights, whose refuge will be the mountain fortress' (Isa. 33:15–6). Then you will be doing what the Lord has commanded you to do. '. . . let your light shine before men, that they may see your good deeds and praise your Father in heaven' (Matt. 5:16). Then you will also be following in the footsteps of the apostle Paul and all other faithful preachers who do not preach themselves but Christ Jesus as Lord (see 2 Cor. 4:5), and who do not seek their own interests, but those of Jesus Christ (see Phil. 2:21). This is the basis on which you, like them, will be greeted with the following words, 'Well done, good and faithful servant! You have been faithful with a few things; I will put you in charge of many things. Come and share your master's happiness!' (Matt. 25:21).

So if I find something in the saints which is worthy of praise and admiration, when I examine it in the clear light of truth, it is really someone else who is worthy of the praise, and so I praise God in his saints. Take, for example, Elisha and the great prophet Elijah, who both brought dead people back to life. This did not happen through their own power, but as a result of the ministry that had been entrusted to them. They achieved new and unprecedented marvels through God dwelling in them performing these marvellous deeds. In himself God is invisible and unapproachable, but he makes himself visible and able to be praised through his saints. God alone is the One who should be praised since he alone is the One who does these wonderful things. 'Praise be to the Lord God, the God of Israel, who alone does marvellous deeds' (Ps. 72:18). Painting and writing are both arts worthy of praise, yet it is not the pen or the brush that should be praised. Neither should praise be given to the lips and tongue which deliver an eloquent speech. The prophet Isaiah spoke the truth when he said, 'Does the axe raise itself above him who swings it, or the saw boast against him who uses it? As if a rod were to wield him who lifts it up, or a club brandish him who is not wood!' (Isa. 10:15).

So anyone who does not give glory to God is in fact detracting from God. 'Let him who boasts boast in the Lord' (2 Cor. 10:17). If it is necessary that a person should glory, the apostle Paul teaches us whom we should glory and how this should be done. He says, 'Now this is our boast: Our conscience testifies that we have conducted ourselves in the world, and especially in our relations with you, in the holiness and sincerity that are from God. We have done so not according to worldly wisdom but according to God's grace' (2 Cor. 1:12). I can glory without fearing that I am doing anything wrong so long as my conscience is testifying that I am not detracting from the glory of my Creator. I can do this with a clear conscience when I am not doing this against the Lord but am doing it in the Lord. We are not forbidden to take part in this kind of glory, but, on the contrary, we are encouraged to engage in it. Our Lord himself said, 'How can you believe if you accept praise from one another, yet make no effort to obtain the praise that comes from the only God?' (John 5:44). In fact, the ability to glory in God alone comes from God alone.

Sermon 14

Conversion – the personal experience of the preacher

I am not ashamed to confess that I frequently experienced extreme coldness and hardness of heart, especially at the beginning of my conversion. I searched for him whom my soul longed to love, but it was not then able to love whom it had not yet found. At least, it loved less than he wished to and for this reason was seeking him so that it might love him more deeply. The soul would definitely not have searched for God without already having experienced his love to a certain extent. So I searched for God while my spirit was frozen and languid and longed to be warmed and find rest. But I found that nobody came alongside me to help me melt the icy lethargy of my spiritual senses or to return the sweetness and fruitfulness of the spring. During this time my soul languished and drooped into lethargy and was prey to strong and hopeless depression as well as full of discontent. When this happened I would murmur to myself, 'Who can withstand his icy blast?' (Ps. 147:17).

Then, all of a sudden, through a word, or the sight of some holy and pious person or the mere thought of a dead person or someone absent, the Holy Spirit would breathe on my frozen soul and the waters would begin to flow. During this time tears were my food both day and night. This was nothing other than the perfume breathed out through the anointing by which the Holy One was invested. It was not the anointing itself which had this effect on me, as the actual anointing did not come to me except through the agency of some person. The gift did give me great joy, but I was confounded and humiliated to know that I enjoyed this delight only for a brief moment and that the source of the blessing had not been given to me. As I could only enjoy this blessing from a distance, and could not come close to it and touch it, I realised that God would not give me its sweetness because of my unworthiness. If the same thing happens to me now I receive whatever blessing I am given with gratitude. I grieve that I was not worthy to be given this gift, from the Lord's hand to my hand, as it were, as I had earnestly requested. I am ashamed that I was more greatly moved through remembering man than through remembering God.

Then I cry with groans, 'When can I go and meet with God?' (Ps. 42:2). I think that some of you have been through, and some are in the middle of, a similar experience. What are we to think about this? God is allowing this experience to warn us of our pride, or to help us persevere in our humility, or to make us more loving to others or to increase our desire for holiness.

Sermon 15

The name of Jesus

Where do you think that such a bright, unexpected and global light of faith has come from, except through the preaching of the name of Jesus? Is it not through the light of this sacred name that God has called us into his marvellous light, so that as we are enlightened by it we also see light? As the apostle Paul was enabled to say to us, 'For you were once in darkness, but now you are light in the Lord' (Eph. 5:8). It was this same name that Paul was told to speak before Gentiles and kings, 'This man is my chosen instrument to carry my name before the Gentiles and their kings and before the people of Israel' (Acts 9:15). Paul bore this name as a lamp which enlightened his country and his people, as he cried everywhere, 'The night is nearly over; the day is almost here. So let us put aside the deeds of darkness and put on the armour of light. Let us behave decently, as in the daytime' (Rom. 13:12–13). To everyone Paul displayed this lamp, set up on its lampstand, when he preached Jesus Christ and him crucified, everywhere he went.

How resplendent that light was; how it dazzled the eyes of everyone who saw it! This light came as a flash of lightning from Peter's mouth as it gave the lame man strong and sound limbs again and as it gave sight to many people who were spiritually blind. Did not this light shine out as a flash of fire when Peter said, 'In the name of Jesus Christ of Nazareth, walk' (Acts 3:6).

The name of Jesus is not only light, it is also nourishing

food. Do you not feel spiritually strengthened every time you meditate on the name of Jesus? What can enrich the mind of a philospher as much as the name of Jesus? What revives exhausted powers, strengthens the soul in all virtues, enables it to do good deeds and fosters a pure and holy outlook in the same way as the name of Jesus can? If the sweet oil of the name of Jesus is not poured over your spiritual food it remains dry and tasteless and as insipid as food that has not been seasoned with salt. A book or a document has nothing worthwhile in it as far as I am concerned if it does not mention the name of Jesus. I have no interest in conferences where the name of Jesus is not heard. Like honey is to the mouth, melodious music to the ear and a song to the heart so is the name of Jesus to the soul.

The name of Jesus is also a medicine. Is there anyone among you who is sad? Let Jesus come into your heart. Let his name leap up to your lips, and like the rising of the sun, let his light disperse the clouds of your sadness and restore your serenity and peace. Is there anyone among you who is turning to crime or even contemplating suicide? Let him call on the life-giving name of Jesus who will quickly revive you. For all the diseases of your soul there is one remedy. What I am saying is proved by the following words, 'call upon me in the day of trouble; I will deliver you' (Ps. 50:15).

There is nothing that is as powerful as the name of Jesus to restrain anger, pride, envy, sinful human passion, avarice and impure thoughts. When I keep the name of Jesus in my mind I think of him as both a human being and the divine God. As a human being Jesus is meek, humble, pure, merciful and full of every quality any saint might possess. As the almighty God Jesus gives me back my spiritual health through his example and makes me strong with his power. I think of all of this when I hear the name of Jesus. His cure is more effective than any prescription from a human doctor.

Sermon 20

Three ways in which we love God

It has been said that Christ's love is tender, wise and strong. 'I say that it is tender, since he has taken on himself our human nature; wise because he has kept himself free from all sin; and strong because he came to the point of enduring death.'

From the way in which Christ lived you can learn, Christian friend, how you should love Christ. Learn to love him tenderly, to love him wisely and to love him with strong powerful love. If you love Christ tenderly you will not be enticed away from him; if you love Christ wisely you will not be deceived and so drawn away from him; if you love Christ powerfully nothing will be able to separate you from him. Take delight in Christ for he is wisdom above everything else. Then human glory and sinful human passions will not take you away from him. Let Christ, who is the truth, so enlighten you that you are not drawn away from him by any false spirit.

Let Christ, who is the power of God, strengthen you so that you are not overcome by any enemies. Let Christian love strengthen your desire to do good; let Christ's wisdom rule you and direct your life and let steadfastness make you persevere in this. Your Christian love must not be lukewarm, timid or indiscreet. This is what is laid down in the Law, when God says, 'Love the Lord your God with all your heart and with all your soul and with all your strength' (Deut. 6:5).

It seems to me that the best way to make the distinctions

57

between the different ways to love God is as follows: the love of the heart concerns your feelings, the love of the soul centres on the decisions of your mind and the love of your strength focuses on the steadfastness of your mind. So you must love the Lord your God wholeheartedly, singlemindedly and sacrificially. As it is written in a later verse in the Song of Songs, 'love is as strong as death, its jealousy unyielding as the grave' (S. of S. 8:6).

Let the Lord Jesus be a delight to your heart so that the false attractions of the sensual life are destroyed. Let Christ's sweetness overcome bodily desires just as one nail drives out another nail. As far as your understanding is concerned let the Lord Jesus be your wise leader. This will enable you to avoid the heretical traps that are set to ensnare you and warp your faith. With Jesus as your guiding light you will be able to avoid excesses and indiscretions. When your faith is steadfast you will not give way to fear or be overcome by suffering. Finally, we must love God in a tender, wise and ardent way. For we know that the love of the heart that goes by the name of tender can be easily led astray if it is not accompanied by the love of the soul. And these two loves need to be reinforced by a strong love if the love is not just going to evaporate.

You will be able to see in the following examples that what I have said is true. The disciples were dismayed when they heard, shortly before the Ascension, their Master speaking about his departure from them, when he said to them, 'If you loved me, you would be glad that I am going to the Father' (John 14:28). Why were they dismayed? Did they not love the One over whose departure they were upset? In a certain sense they did love him, and yet they did not really love him. That is, the disciples loved Jesus tenderly, but not wisely. They loved in a human way but not in a spiritual way. They loved him with their hearts but not with their souls. Their love was against the best interests of their own salvation, as Jesus was later to say to them, 'It is for your good that I am going away' (John 16:7). Jesus put the blame of their deficient love on their lack of wisdom and not on their feelings of love for him.

When Jesus spoke about his impending death, you will remember that it was Peter, who loved Jesus, who tried to stop him from going through with it. Jesus reprimanded Peter in his reply, but did so in a way that showed that he was only blaming him for his lack of prudence. What do you think is the purpose of the words, 'You do not have in mind the things of God, but the things of men' (Mark 8:33)? Jesus is telling Peter that he is not loving wisely, but just from a human point of view. Jesus even said, 'Get behind me, Satan! (Mark 8:33). Here Jesus tells Peter that, without realising it, he is being totally unwise and even an enemy of salvation if he were to prevent the Saviour from being crucified. The next time Jesus made a prediction about his death Peter did not oppose him, but said that he was willing to die beside him. But Peter was not able to carry out that promise because he had not reached the third stage of love for God, which consists in loving God with all our strength. Peter had learned to love God with his soul, but he was still weak. Peter knew what he ought to do, but he did not have the strength to do it. He was not ignorant about the mystery of salvation, but he shrank from martyrdom. This love that Peter showed was clearly not as strong as death as it had collapsed with fear when it was faced with death. This position changed later on when Peter, in line with Jesus Christ's promise, was given power from God. Then Peter was enabled to love with such great courage that he preached the name of Jesus even though he had been forbidden to do so by the council. He even replied to them firmly when they told him to stop with these words, 'We must obey God rather than men!' (Acts 5:29).

At last, Peter was loving God with all his strength, for Peter did not spare his own life on account of his love for God. 'Greater love has no-one than this, that he lay down his life for his friends' (John 15:13). He was prepared to sacrifice his life at that moment, although he was not, in

59

the event, called upon to do so. When we are not diverted from our love for God by flattery, tricks or persecution, then we are loving God with all our mind, all our soul and all our strength.

Notice that the love of the heart is in one sense human, in that the heart of man is moved by Christ's human life and the commands he gave while he was here on earth. Anyone who is filled with this love will be open to be moved when he hears about the things which Christ did during his lifetime. He revels in nothing more than listening to the gospel stories about Jesus, reading them carefully and bringing them to his mind. His sacrifices of prayer are lifted on to a higher plane and his sacrifices become, as it were, as meaty as they are beautiful. Every time he prays the image of the God-man comes before him as he recalls Christ's birth, infancy, teachings, death, Resurrection or Ascension. These, and other similar pictures of Christ in his mind, animate his soul and fill it with a desire for holiness, as well as expelling sensual vices and temptations. God, who is invisible, planned that he should be seen as a man and live among men so that he could attract the love of human beings to his humanity. Human beings who could love only in a human way were then led on from this to love God in a spiritual way. The people who said to Jesus, 'We have left everything to follow you!' (Matt. 19:27) were still at the first stage of love for God. They had left everything for the human person of Jesus. This is why they could not calmly listen to him speaking about his impending Passion and death. Even later on they were deeply saddened to look on Jesus disappearing to heaven at his Ascension. For this reason Jesus said to them, 'Because I have said these things you are filled with grief' (John 16:6).

In the meantime Jesus had drawn them away and kept them from all human desires by the grace of his personal presence as a human being.

Later on Jesus pointed out to them a higher degree of love, when he said, 'The Spirit gives life; the flesh counts for nothing' (John 6:63). This higher degree of love is reflected in the following words of the apostle Paul, 'So from now on we regard no-one from a worldly point of view. Though we once regarded Christ in this way, we do so no longer' (2 Cor. 5:16). If I prefer any human relationships to my Lord is it not clear that I am not loving him with all my heart? I have a divided heart because I give some love to Christ and some for myself. Did not Jesus himself say, 'Anyone who loves his father or mother more than me is not worthy of me; anyone who loves his son or daughter more than me is not worthy of me' (Matt. 10:37)? So, to put it briefly, to love Jesus with the whole heart is to prefer the love of his human life above everything else that may engage my feelings, whether such feelings come from myself or from other people. In this sense the glory of the world is equally dangerous to your soul as it is full of human desires. People who take delight in the world are undoubtedly absorbed by sinful human desires.

This devotion to the humanity of Christ is a great gift from the Holy Spirit. And yet I have to label this love as sinful human desire when it is compared with other more spiritual desires. For it is possible to seek after Christian graces, such as wisdom, righteousness, holiness and goodness, in the power of mere human effort. The way to remedy this is to recall these words of Paul, 'It is because of him that you are in Christ Jesus, who has become for us wisdom from God – that is, our righteousness, holiness and redemption' (1 Cor. 1:30).

It can seem that two people have an equal love for Christ. The first person is saddened by Christ's sufferings, is moved to Godly repentance by them and is affected when he recalls all the sufferings of Christ. He draws spiritual strength from Christ's Passion and death and is enabled to carry out good deeds as a result. The second person is always zealous about being righteous, has a great passion for the truth, earnestly desires God's wisdom and above all else seeks to live a holy life which is characterised by perfectly disciplined behaviour. This person is ashamed at ostentation, abhors being detracted away from God, is not envious of other people, detests pride and not only avoids but dislikes and despises all kinds of worldly glory. This person really hates and sets out to destroy in himself every kind of impurity in his heart and mind. He has a natural inclination to reject evil and embrace all that is good. If you compare these two types of love for God do you not clearly see that the second is superior to the first? When the first person is compared with the second person it is clear that the first person's life is lived in a human, sinful way.

Yet the love which shuts out human, sinful living and condemns and overcomes the world is good, although it remains human love. As it makes more progress it moves on to being rational love and when it is perfected it becomes spiritual love. This love can be termed rational when all thoughts about Christ are in line with the teaching of the Church and are not heretical in any way. Our personal behaviour has to be transformed so that we are devoid of superstition, levity and anything else that belongs to our fallen human nature. When we do this we are loving God with all our soul. When we love God's Son so strongly, through the help of the powerful Holy Spirit, that we do not stop seeking God's righteousness in the midst of troubles, sufferings or the threat of death, then we are loving God with all our strength. This love is spiritual love. Spiritual love is a particularly apt name to give to this kind of love because its characteristic is the fullness of the Spirit. I think that this is all I need to say about the bride's words, 'No wonder the maidens love you!' (S. of S. 1:3).

Sermon 28

Hearing, rather than sight, prevails in matters of faith and in the knowledge of the truth

'How beautiful!' The man who exclaimed, 'Truly this man was the Son of God', had surely perceived. The centurion who saw Christ die had seen something. What he saw we must now examine. For if the centurion had perceived only what everyone else saw why should he praise God and call him the Son of God or beautiful? What else was there to observe other than a tortured, repulsive body that had been nailed to the cross with outstretched hands between two robbers, was subject to degrading jeers and was wept over by faithful followers? The one person who had the right to be revered was the object of laughter.

Where did the centurion come under the spell of the crucified Christ? Where did he learn that the man who was numbered with the transgressors was really the Son of God? It is not necessary for me to answer that question as the evangelist has done this. These are his words, 'And when the centurion, which stood over against him, saw that he so cried out, and gave up the ghost, he said, Truly this man was the Son of God' (Mark 15:39 AV). So the centurion believed when he heard Christ's voice and he did not believe on account of what he saw. So do you not think that he was one of the sheep who follow the man who enters by the gate? Speaking of this man (himself) Jesus said, 'his sheep follow him because they know his voice'

(John 10:4).

Through hearing, a truth is discovered which does not reach us through our sight. Appearances can deceive our eyes while truth enters through the ear. The eye declared that Christ was weak, defiled, miserable and condemned to the most ignominious of deaths. However, the ear understands that this person was the Son of God and that he was altogether beautiful. But these ears did not belong to the Jews who were uncircumcised in their hearing. It was not without reason that St Peter cut off the ear of the high priest's servant. He did it as if he was trying to make a way in for the truth. Then he would have discovered what Jesus said to the Jews who had believed in him, 'Then you will know the truth, and the truth will set you free' (John 8:32).

The centurion was not circumcised, but he was circumcised in his hearing as he was able to recognise the Lord, despite his many weaknesses through a single sentence of a dying man. He did not despise what Jesus said because he believed in what he was unable to see. He did not even believe because of what he could see, but on the contrary, he believed without wavering on account of what he heard. '. . . Faith comes from hearing' (Rom. 10:17). It would have indeed been worthy of the truth if it had entered the soul through the eyes, as the eyes are its windows, and its more important sense. But, my soul, the eyes are reserved for the time when we shall see God face to face. In the meantime, it is good that the remedy for our spiritual illness should enter in through the same way as the disease itself came in to us and that life should come after death and tread hard on its heels. It is right that light should come after the darkness and that the serpent's poison should be followed by the truth, which is the cure for the poison. When the eye that was unwell is cured it can then look at Christ, whom it was previously unable to see because of its lack of sight. Death entered first of all through the ear so it is appropriate that it should now be the first way in for life. The hearing that was originally

64

responsible for taking away sight can now restore sight. For if we do not believe in God's mysteries we shall never be able to understand them. So hearing is the way in which we understand about salvation and seeing God will be our reward for faith in God. This is why the Psalmist says, 'Let me hear joy and gladness' (Ps. 51:8). The reward for listening to God faithfully is the blessed vision and one deserves that blessed vision through faithful hearing.

Our Lord says, 'Blessed are the pure in heart, for they will see God' (Matt. 5:8). For any eye to see God it has to be purified by faith, as St Peter said, 'he [God] purified their hearts by faith' (Acts 15:9).

Until our sight is ready to perceive God our sense of hearing must be aroused and used to receive the truth. Happy are the people about whom it can be truly said, 'As soon as they hear me, they obey me' (Ps. 18:44). I shall be worthy of looking at God so long as I have obeyed him before I try to look at him. When God has received my sacrifice of obedience I shall be able to look at him with confidence. How happy is the man who says, 'The Sovereign Lord has opened my ears, and I have not been rebellious; I have not drawn back' (Isa. 50:5).

Here you have a model of voluntary obedience, an example of perseverance. For anybody who, of his own accord, does not stop doing good deeds can go on to persevere in them. The willingness to do good deeds and perseverance in doing the good deeds are both necessary. This is seen because, 'God loves a cheerful giver' (2 Cor. 9:7), and because 'he who stands firm to the end will be saved' (Matt. 10:22). May the Lord deign to open my ears as well so that the word of truth may enter my heart, purify my eyes and prepare them for the joyful vision of himself, so that I can say to him, 'You hear, O Lord, the desire of the afflicted' (Ps. 10:17). Along with all others who obey God I want to hear him say, 'You are already clean because of the word I have spoken to you' (John 15:3). Not everyone who listens to his Word is made

65

clean, only those who obey it: 'Blessed rather are those who hear the word of God and obey it' (Luke 11:28). God requires us to listen to him in the same way that he required the people of Israel to listen to him, 'Hear, O Israel, and be careful to obey so that it may go well with you and that you may increase greatly in a land flowing with milk and honey, just as the Lord, the God of your fathers, promised you' (Deut. 6:3). This kind of hearing is seen in the following quotation from the book of Samuel, 'Speak, Lord, for your servant is listening' (1 Sam. 3:9). The Psalmist is a good example to follow in this respect, 'I will listen to what God the Lord will say' (Ps. 85:8).

The Holy Spirit also follows this principle as far as making progress in the spiritual life is concerned. The Holy Spirit desires that you are in the habit of listening to him before he gives the soul spiritual insight. Take note of what is said in one of the Psalms, 'Listen, O daughter, consider and give ear' (Ps. 45:10). Why do you open your eyes when what you should be doing is to open your ears! Do you really want to see Christ? Then, the first thing that you have to do is to listen to what is said about him so that you may say when you do see him, 'As we have heard, so have we seen' (Ps. 48:8). The brightness of this vision of Christ cannot be measured and yet your vision is so feeble that you cannot see anything. You may, perhaps, be able to hear his words, but you are not able to look at him. When I was a sinner I heard God calling Adam in the garden, 'Where are you?' (Gen. 3:9), but I did not see God. If your hearing is humble and faithful it will restore your sight. Faith will purify your eye which became diseased through ungodliness. Whereas disobedience closed your eyes obedience can open them again. Lastly, the truth of the matter is as the Psalmist has said, 'I gain understanding from your precepts' (Ps. 119:104). The observance of God's commands restores our understanding which had become warped because we broke these commands.

Think about the good man Isaac, who, when he was

very elderly, retained his powers of hearing, even though he lost his other senses. The eyesight of the patriarch was poor, his sense of taste was impaired, his sense of feeling in his hands deceived him, but his hearing remained strong. Was it not wonderful that he could still hear since, 'faith comes from hearing the message, and the message is heard through the word of Christ' (Rom. 10:17)? The voice he heard was Jacob's, and he was correct; but the hands he felt were Esau's hands and he had been deceived here. You can be so wrong, as the similarity of the feel of a hand can deceive you. Your sense of taste is not a reliable guide about the truth, even though it can tell you what it enjoys. Is it telling you the truth when you think that you are eating venison when in reality you are eating the meat of a tame kid? You should not place any confidence in your poor eyesight as it is unable to perceive either truth or wisdom. The prophet says, 'Woe to those who are wise in their own eyes' (Isa. 5:21). It is not genuine wisdom that is being condemned here, rather, it is 'the wisdom of this world' which 'is foolishness in God's sight' (1 Cor. 3:19), that is being condemned.

True wisdom comes from within and is hidden as godly Job discovered. Why do you seek wisdom from outside and from your bodily senses? Taste comes from the palate whereas wisdom is from the heart. Do not seek wisdom with your human eye for flesh and blood do not reveal wisdom, only the Spirit does. Wisdom is not found through taste for, 'it cannot be found in the land of the living' (Job 28:13). Wisdom does not come from any touch of the hand, for as Job also says, 'my hand offered them a kiss of homage, then these also would be sins to be judged, for I would have been unfaithful to God on high' (Job 31:27–8).

I believe that this is the case when God's gift of wisdom is not attributed to God, but to some human action. Even though Isaac was a wise man his senses led him astray. Is truth only to be found in hearing? Yes, this is the case, because the word of God is perceived through hearing.

67

The woman in the gospel record was correctly forbidden to touch the human body of the risen Word because she sought only after human wisdom. She placed more trust in her eyes than in the oracles of God. She preferred her human senses to the word of God. She did not believe that the One whom she had seen die was raised to life again, even though Jesus himself had promised that it would happen in this way. Her eyes were not content with seeing Jesus because she found no comfort through faith or in God's promises. Are not heaven and earth, as well as everything that can be seen by the human eye, destined to be destroyed before one jot or tittle of all that God has said is fulfilled? This woman refused to be consoled by the Word of the Lord and yet she stopped crying as soon as she saw Jesus because she placed more importance on the experience of her senses than on the certainty of faith. But this kind of experience is deceptive.

We return to this event with the certain knowledge of faith which is able to understand things that the senses can never fathom and which they have never experienced. 'Do not hold on to me' (John 20:17) the Saviour says. He is saying, Stop relying on your human senses which can be so easily deceived and put your trust in my Word and become used to exercising faith in this way. Faith cannot be deceived. Faith does not feel the poverty which is characteristic of the senses, but faith is able to understand invisible things and can pass beyond human reasoning and beyond everything that the senses can experience. So why do you demand from the eye what it is incapable of giving you? And why do you expect from the hand what it is not capable of telling you? Whatever information these senses bring you is inferior to the understanding of faith. Faith reveals truth about Jesus Christ which is the most important thing in the world. You must learn to hold with a firmer grasp and follow with greater confidence whatever faith tells you. 'Jesus said, "Do not hold on to me, for I have not yet returned to the Father"' (John 20:17). Jesus said this as if he could only be touched by and desired by Mary after he had ascended. Yet, he could undoubtedly be touched even before his ascension, but only by the heart, not by the hands; by prayer not by sight; by faith and not by human senses.

'Why,' says the risen Lord Jesus, 'do you want to touch me now since you only appreciate the glory of my resurrection through your physical senses? Do you not remember when I lived with you that my disciples were unable to view my glory for one moment during my transfiguration? At present you can still see me partially with your senses while I have this servant's body. But my glory is wonderful and totally beyond you so that you are unable to reach it in any way.' So you must suspend your judgment and not rely on your senses in such an important matter which can only be correctly appreciated through faith. Faith helps you fully to understand this as it is through faith that profound mystical truths are plumbed. Faith can understand the height, the depth, the length and the breadth of the mystery of God's love. '. . . as it is written: "No eye has seen, no ear has heard, no mind has conceived what God has prepared for those who love him"' (1 Cor. 2:9). Faith can reveal to you what lies under an impenetrable covering as far as all your senses are concerned.

So only faith can really touch Jesus and contemplate him, sitting at the right hand of God the Father, as Jesus no longer in the form of a servant but in his heavenly glory as he was before the creation of the world. Why do you desire to touch Jesus before he is glorified? Wait until Jesus is transformed and glorified and then seek to touch him by faith in his perfect and wonderful glory.

The Church complains about her persecutors, those who sow division among Christians

'My mother's sons were angry with me' (S. of S. 1:6). Dear Christian friends, let there be peace among you. Do not cause pain to anyone else through your words, actions or even your slightest bodily movements in case one of you becomes embittered and preoccupied about his own weak spirit. Because of the sufferings he is put through he asks God to come to his rescue from the grip of those who are hurting him. He has this very serious complaint against them, 'My mother's sons were angry with me'. When you sin against your Christian brother you are sinning against Christ. Christ said, 'I tell you the truth, whatever you did for one of the least of these brothers of mine, you did for me' (Matt. 25:40).

It is not good enough just to be innocent of the most grave offences in this area, such as open insults and abuse, you must not be guilty of secret poisonous whispers against anybody. I must repeat, it is not enough to guard our lips against these and other kinds of fault because even the smallest injury to someone else must be avoided. We should not really call any fault small if it is committed with the deliberate intention of harming a brother. As our Saviour has said, 'anyone who is angry with his brother will be subject to judgment' (Matt. 5:22).

This is absolutely correct because what you may consider to be a small thing, and therefore indulge in without the slightest hesitation, the person against whom you inflict the injury views it in a totally different light. You are acting just like a person who only looks on the surface of things, judges everything according to appearances, thinks that a splinter is a plank of wood and a single spark is a raging fire. The kind of Christian love which believes all things is absent from the heart of this kind of person. For the spirit of men and the thoughts of their hearts are inclined to suspect evil rather than to think good things. This is particularly the case where the rule of silence prevents you, whose conduct is questionable, from excusing yourself, and does not allow the person who suspects you of harming him to speak about what he rightly feels you have done, and so clear up the matter.

Inwardly he is on fire, he feels as if he is going to die, he groans within himself because he is totally preoccupied with anger. He cannot concentrate on anything other than the injury he has sustained. He cannot pray, he cannot read or meditate on any holy or spiritual subjects. This soul, for whom Christ died, travels along the way that leads to death and is cut off from all the influence of the life-giving Spirit and is deprived of his benefits. While this is happening, I ask you, what is the state of your mind? What pleasure can you take in prayer, in work, or in any task that you might be engaged in? What frame of mind are you in? You have made your brother's heart sad and Christ cries out in anxiety for him. Jesus says, 'My mother's sons are fighting against me', and, 'The person who has eaten of the delights of my table has filled me with bitterness.'

If you reply that your brother should not trouble himself so deeply over such a small matter, I reply that the smaller the offence the easier it is for you to avoid it. However, I do not know how you can call any injury slight (as I have already said) which is the cause for making someone else angry. You know from the lips of the Judge himself that this puts you in danger of being condemned. Do you think that it is a small matter which offends Christ

71

and for which you are brought into judgment? 'It is a dreadful thing to fall into the hands of the living God' (Heb. 10:31).

When you are on the receiving end of some injury, as will inevitably be the case (for it is difficult to prevent such a thing happening in a community like this), do not behave in the way of the world and quickly get back at your brother with a hostile answer. Do not make any retaliation, under the guise of a reply, which involves cutting words which make deep wounds in a soul for whom Christ allowed himself to be crucified. Do not give a sour reply, or grumble under your breath, or sneer in your manner, or laugh in a mocking way or frown as if you were angry and threatening your brother. Let your anger die down completely as soon as it is born. Do not allow it even to show itself because it brings death in its wake and it may even kill some soul. Then you will be able to say with the Psalmist, 'I was too troubled to speak' (Ps. 77:4).

Sermon 31

The vision of God. How, at present, the delight in the divine presence experienced by godly people varies according to the different desires of their souls

'Tell me, you whom I love, where you graze your flock and where you rest your sheep at midday' (S. of S. 1:7). The Word, who is the Bridegroom, frequently appears to zealous souls but not only in one kind of appearance. Why is that? Undoubtedly it is because we cannot yet see him as he is. 'Dear friends, now we are children of God, and what we will be has not yet been made known. But we know that when he appears, we shall be like him, for we shall see him as he is' (1 John 3:2). The vision of Christ that we shall have in heaven will last because the state in which we see him then will be everlasting. For Christ is, and he does not change on account of anything that is, or has been, or will be. If you take away the past and the future, what room is there left for any change? Everything which changes from being what it was into what it will be passes through some point of existence even though it does not exist. For how can we say that something 'is' which never remains in the same state? So the only person who really 'is' is the person who is neither cut off from the past nor obliterated from the future, but remains alone, unchanging. Because he has not been he is from all eternity. Because he will not be he exists for all eternity. So Christ truly exists and is uncreated, without limit and unchangeable. When Christ, who apparently is not in this or that mode of existence, is seen, he is not changed by anything else. Christ is then the one and the same 'denarius' (see Matt. 20:9) which we read of in the gospel which is given to everyone who sees him in this way, as he is presented to them only in this way.

Christ is unchangeable in himself and he is present with no change to those who view him. People who do see the vision of Christ neither desire to see, nor are capable of seeing anything more delightful than this. So how can their eager gaze be satisfied, their delight fulfilled or their search for truth rewarded? This can happen only in eternity. For if the will to look at Christ and the ability to look at Christ are both enlarged in eternity nothing will be lacking to bring complete happiness. Nothing else remains to be experienced or desired by those people who always desire to look at Christ and in whom that desire is being eternally satisfied.

But such a beatific vision is not for this present life because it is reserved for our final state of existence, for those who can at least say, 'we know that when he appears, we shall be like him, for we shall see him as he is' (1 John 3:2).

During this present life Christ appears to whom he wishes in the state that he chooses, rather than appearing in the state that he exists. No living person, no matter how holy or wise he may be, and no prophet is able or has ever been able to see Christ as he is. People who will be deemed worthy of seeing Christ will do so when they have immortal bodies. So Christ is indeed seen, but in a way that he says is best and he is not seen as he is. For although you view that great light (I am referring to the sun which you see every day), you have never really seen it, you just see the things that it lights up – things like the air, or a wall or a mountain. You would be unable even to see it in this inferior way if the light of your body, your eye, did not in some way approximate to the light of heaven in its innate clearness and serenity. No other part of the body is able to recognise light as every other part of the body is so different from the eye. When the eye is unwell it is not able to receive light. When the eye is disturbed it is unable to look at the sun, which remains peaceful, because the eye is so unlike the sun in this respect. But when it is peaceful it is able to see the sun with clear, untroubled vision. If the eye was as pure as the object it looked at it would not be dazzled because of the great similarity between them both.

In the same way the person who is enlightened by the Sun of Righteousness who 'gives light to every man' (John 1:9) that comes into the world is able to look at Christ to the extent that he has been enlighted by him and so is like him. Because no person is perfectly like Christ nobody can see Christ perfectly. This is why the Psalmist says, 'Those who look to him are radiant; their faces are never covered with shame' (Ps. 34:5). This is indeed the case, so long as we are enlightened as much as we need to be. But we all with open face beholding as in a glass the glory of the Lord, are changed into the same image from glory to glory, even as by the Spirit of the Lord 'which comes from the Lord, who is the Spirit' (2 Cor. 3:18).

So we must never approach God carelessly or irreverently, but with respect and awe for fear that an irreverent person will be crushed and destroyed by Christ's glory. We are not to suppose that we can approach him more easily by coming to him in different places. We have to become more worthy of seeing God, not through our body but in our spiritual lives as the Spirit of the Lord is our guide. It is through the Lord's Spirit that we draw near to Christ and not through our own spirit although it is in our own spirit that all this happens. So the purer and more virtuous a spirit is the nearer it is to God and if a spirit reaches complete purity and is wholly virtuous it enters into the very presence of God. To be in God's presence is to see him as he is and this takes place when the human spirit is totally like God and so is not dazzled by God's presence as he is not unlike him. But, as I have said, this happens only in heaven. In our present existence there is a wide variety of created beings. They obtain their existence from the rays of the divine Sun although they are not able completely to see who God is.

So you are able to see some things about God, but you cannot see God himself. When you do perceive something of God, even though you cannot see God, you are nevertheless assured that he does exist and that ought to lead you on to seek him.

The person who seeks God will receive God's grace to do this while the person who does not bother to do this will not be able to use the excuse that he cannot seek God because of his ignorance. This way of understanding is common in all rational creatures. 'For', says the apostle Paul, 'since the creation of the world God's invisible qualities – his eternal power and divine nature – have been clearly seen, being understood from what has been made, so that men are without excuse' (Rom. 1:20).

God doubtless revealed himself to the patriarchs in another way as he gave them frequent fellowship of his presence with them. But even here God was not actually seen by them, although he did make himself known. God did not just make himself known to them on one single occasion, for the letter to the Hebrews says, 'In the past God spoke to our forefathers through the prophets at many times and in various ways' (Heb. 1:1). Of course, in himself, 'The Lord our God, the Lord is one' (Deut. 6:4), as he declared to Israel.

This revelation was not given to everyone, although it came from outside and was visible to the senses and could be heard by ears. But there was another way in which God is known which differs from this because

God is also known inwardly. God revealed himself in this way to souls who searched for him. On these seeking souls God lavished his entire love and affection. This is evidence that God has come to a soul as we know from the Psalmist who experienced this for himself, 'Fire goes before him and consumes his foes on every side' (Ps. 97:3). It is necessary that all evil deeds and impure thoughts should be eradicated from the soul which is longing to be sanctified as it presents itself in God's presence. When the soul perceives that the Lord is close by and feels itself being consumed by the flames of its longing it says, 'From on high he sent fire, sent it down into my bones' (Lam. 1:13), and, 'My heart grew hot within me, and as I meditated, the fire burned' (Ps. 39:3).

A soul may press towards God in this way, or perhaps through constant prayer, and experience the pain of its longings after God. In the middle of this, God sometimes has pity on the soul that is seeking him so earnestly and reveals himself to it. When this does happen the soul can unite with Jeremiah and say, 'The Lord is good to those whose hope is in him, to the one who seeks him' (Lam. 3:25).

God's angel, who is one of the companions of the Bridegroom, has been commissioned to watch over this individual soul. The angel ministers to the soul and greatly rejoices as it witnesses the soul's communion with God. Turning to the Lord, the angel says, 'I thank you, O God of infinite majesty, because you have granted the earnest desires of that soul and you have not rejected the request of his mouth.'

This angel goes everywhere with the soul that has been committed to its care and continually encourages it and warns it as it says: 'Delight yourself in the Lord and he will give you the desires of your heart' (Ps. 37:4); and, 'Be still before the Lord and wait patiently for him' (Ps. 37:7); and, 'Though it linger, wait for it; it will certainly come and will not delay' (Hab. 2:3). Then the

77

angel speaks to the Lord and says, 'As the deer pants for streams of water, so my soul pants for you, O God' (Ps 42:1); and, 'My soul yearns for you in the night; in the morning my spirit longs for you' (Isa. 26:9); and, 'I call to you, O Lord, every day; I spread out my hands to you' (Ps. 88:9); and, 'Send her away, for she keeps crying out after us' (Matt. 15:23); and 'Relent, O Lord! How long will it be? Have compassion on your servants' (Ps. 90:13).

The angel says, 'Look down from heaven, and see and visit that lonely soul. Faithful is the friend of the Bridegroom because he is aware of that mutual love but not jealous about it.' The soul is not seeking its own interest but that of his Lord.

The angel travels between the Bridegroom and the bride, presenting the prayers of one of them and bringing back gifts from the other. One he arouses while the other he appeases. Occasionally he brings the one to be introduced to the other. For the angel is God's servant, living in God's house, and every day he looks at the Father's face and he never fears that his requests will be refused.

Be careful that you do not think that there is anything either imaginary or in bodily form about the Word mixing with the believer's soul. I am only saying what the apostle Paul said, 'he who unites himself with the Lord is one with him in spirit' (1 Cor. 6:17). I go on to express, as best as I am able, how a pure soul is absorbed into God, or how the Holy God comes down to a soul, as I compare spiritual things with spiritual things. This union takes place in the Spirit because God is Spirit. God is moved with love for the beauty of that soul which he may have seen walking according to the Spirit, having no desire to fulfil the lusts of the flesh, especially since God knows that this soul is full of strong longing for him.

A soul that is like that and has such ardent feelings is not content that the Bridegroom should show himself to

78

her in the same way that he reveals himself to everyone else. This soul is not content to receive dreams and visions, which are granted to a few people, as she desires the special privilege that God should come from on high to visit her and pervade her completely in her inner being to the depths of her heart. This soul does not want God, whom she loves, to reveal himself in some outward form, but wants God, as it were, to be poured into her. This soul does not want God just to appear to her, but to come into her and to take her over as she is convinced that she will be much happier if God is inside her and does not just remain outside her. God is the Word and is not just heard by the ears. He penetrates the heart and he does not only enter the ears through the soul's hearing, but enters the feelings with unspeakable delight. The features of God cannot be drawn or defined, but he does nevertheless exercise great power, which although he may not be seen with the eye he still rejoices the heart, not with any beautiful form or colour, but through the feelings which he generates in the soul.

I am unable to describe how God reveals himself, as he really is, to a soul, but God does show himself exactly as he is. However, no matter how completely reverent and devoted a soul may be God will not abide with it permanently nor does God reveal himself in the same way to everyone.

Just as the desires of a soul vary, so the delight of the divine presence also varies. The soul's palate finds the taste of God's heavenly sweetness to vary depending on how much it is seeking after and longing for God. Also, you will have noticed in this song of love how often God has altered his way of appearing and the numerous different forms in which he has made himself known to his beloved. Sometimes he is like a modest wife seeking secretly to enjoy communion with a holy soul and taking pleasure in this devotion. At other times he is more like a doctor who has oils and medicines for weak, tender souls who still need consolation and who are called maidens to indicate their frailty. If anybody objects to this let him remember that 'It is not the healthy who need a doctor, but the sick' (Matt. 9:12). At other times God presents himself as a traveller who accompanies the bride and the young maidens who are walking with her and brings cheer to the whole group on their tiring journey. God talks to them so wonderfully that when he leaves them they say, 'Were not our hearts burning within us while he talked with us on the road?' (Luke 24:32).

God is a most delightful travelling companion because of his actions, his conversation and the wonderful perfume he breathes around him. In this way he leads on those who are following him and therefore they say, 'Pleasing is the fragrance of your perfumes; your name is like perfume poured out' (S. of S. 1:3).

At other times he appears more like the head of some grand family which has a home overflowing with provisions for everyone, or perhaps he is like a powerful king who appears to praise the poverty of his timid bride. This king shows the bride the treasures of his glory and arouses in her a desire for them. Then he shows her his well-stocked wine cellars and granaries until he finally brings her into his inner chamber. For her husband's heart completely wins her and he is sure that none of these things should be hidden from the one he has brought out of poverty whom he now embraces as his beloved friend and to whom he has proved faithful.

God does not limit the kind of inner and spiritual revelations he chooses to lavish on those who see him so that his promise can come true, 'I am with you always, to the very end of the age' (Matt. 28:20).

Throughout all these revelations God is kind, gentle and merciful. His embraces indicate how loving and caring he is, while his oils, perfumes and other medicines point to his forgiving and compassionate nature. As a travelling companion he is found to be cheerful, affable and full of comfort. When he shows his riches he is reminding us about his generous gifts which he has lavished on us.

In this way you find that the Word is depicted in a wide variety of ways all the way through the Song of Songs. This is what I believe that the prophet meant when he said, 'Christ the Lord is a Spirit before our face; under his shadow we will live among the Gentiles' (see Lam. 4:20). However, at present, we can only see dimly through a glass and not yet face to face. But this only lasts while we live among the nations of the world because when we live with the angels it will be different. Then our happiness will be like theirs. Then we shall see God no longer as a poor image of himself, but as he is, in the form of God. As I have already said God had been previously known through these types, but now through the grace of Christ he is present among us in the flesh and the truth shines out through its own light. So we cannot deny that in comparison with the future life our present life is but a shadow of the truth. This must be the case, unless we wish to contradict the apostle Paul when he said, 'For we know in part and we prophesy in part' (1 Cor. 13:9), and also when he said, 'Not that I have already obtained all this, or have already been made perfect, but I press on to take hold of that for which Christ Jesus took hold of me' (Phil. 3:12). This is precisely the difference between those who walk by faith and those who walk by sight. The just must live by faith and those blessed by God in looking at the One they love. Godly people live on earth in the shadow of Christ, while angels delight in his heavenly splendour and in the light of his presence.

Faith may well be but a shadow of the full glory yet to come. It is, however, good as it shades our weak and dull eyes from God's brilliant light. For as it is written, 'he purified their hearts by faith' (Acts 15:9). So faith does not extinguish the light, but preserves it. However great an angel's vision may be, the shadow of faith can preserve it for me. Faith, as it were, wraps the vision in its outstretched arms and reveals the vision to me at the right time. Is it not best for you to possess in a covered and hidden form what you are not capable of receiving in all its uncovered brilliance? Even the mother of the Lord lived in the shadow of faith, for it was said of her, 'Blessed is she who has believed' (Luke 1:45). According to the words of the angel, Mary lived in the shadow cast by the body of Christ, 'the power of the Most High will overshadow you' (Luke 1:35).

This shadow cast by the Most High should not be thought of lightly. There was definitely power in the body of Christ which overshadowed the Virgin Mary so that what is impossible for a mortal woman, sustaining the presence and the unapproachable light of the divine majesty, she was enabled to endure by sheltering under the shadow of that life-giving body. This strength no opposing power could subdue. In his strength Christ puts demons to flight, under his shadow men are safely sheltered. Christ's strength gives power and his shelter provides pleasant coolness.

So we who walk by faith are fed by the body of Christ so that we can live the divine life and we live under Christ's shadow. As Christ said, 'my flesh is real food' (John 6:55). Perhaps this is the reason why Christ is described as a shepherd or pastor, where the bride seems to speak to Christ as if he was one of the shepherds, saying, 'Tell me, you whom I love, where you graze your flock and where you rest your sheep at midday' (S. of S. 1:7). This is the same person who said, 'I am the good shepherd. The good shepherd lays down his life for the sheep' (John 10:11). He gives his life to redeem them and he gives his body to them so that they can be fed. How marvellous this is! Christ is the pastor of the sheep. He provides pasture for the sheep as well as the price for their redemption!

Now this sermon is becoming too long because I am trying to cover such a vast subject which contains so many great truths which cannot be stated in a few words. I must now break off rather than end. As the subject is not finished we must bear in mind that I shall resume where I now leave off and complete it in so far as I am enabled to do so by the Lord Jesus Christ, the Bridegroom of the Church, who is over all, God, blessed for ever. Amen.

Sermon 32

Christ reveals himself to the godly soul as the Bridegroom and to the weak, imperfect soul as the heavenly Doctor

If any of us are like the Psalmist, when he said, 'it is good to be near God' (Ps. 73:28), or to speak more plainly, if any of us are filled with an earnest longing to be with Christ and constantly thirst with great fervour for this we shall undoubtedly receive the Word as the Bridegroom. In that moment he will experience inwardly the loving embrace from the arms of divine wisdom and will receive a delightful inpouring of divine love. Although he is still on his pilgrimage as a human being he will receive the desires of his heart for a brief moment. For when the Lord has been earnestly searched for in watching and in prayers, with many tears, God will eventually present himself to such a soul. So the soul does receive God's presence, but this glides away suddenly.

God visits the soul which seeks after him with tears. God allows himself to be regained, but not to be retained, and, soon, he slips through the hands of the soul. However, if the devout soul perseveres in prayers and tears God will eventually return to it. God will not deprive it of the desire of its lips, even though he does go away again quickly and does not return unless he is sought wholeheartedly. So it is possible in this life to experience the presence of the Bridegroom, even though it is impossible to know the fullness of his presence, since God's presence makes the heart glad, but then the heart is saddened by God's absence.

The beloved has to endure this until she dies and is borne up on the pinions, so to speak, of her earnest desires and starts to fly away. Like a bird she will then glide over the plains of contemplation and follow, without any hindrance, the spirit of her Beloved, wherever he goes.

Nevertheless the Bridegroom will not reveal himself, even for a moment, to every soul. He only reveals himself to souls which show great devotion, earnest desire and tender affection to be his bride. Such souls are fit for the Word in all his beauty to visit him as a Bridegroom. Some souls have not reached this position and still need to repent as they remember their sins, and speak out in bitterness of soul and say to God, 'Do not condemn me' (Job 10:2). These souls may also suffer from strong temptations which draw them away from God and entice them into lust. Such souls are not in need of a Bridegroom but of a heavenly doctor. As this is the case these souls do not receive tenderness from God but oils and medicines to heal their wounds. Is not this the condition in which we often find ourselves as we pray? Are we not every day either tried by our present passions or afflicted with remorse over our previous sins? The appearance in my soul of the good Lord Jesus has often delivered me from such bitter sorrows. How often, after I have poured out my distress with countless tears, sobs and groans have you anointed my wounded conscience with blessing of your mercy and have sprinkled over me the oil of your gladness! How often I have started to pray, almost despairing my salvation and you have sent me back full of joy and with the confidence of your pardon!

People who are also afflicted in this way will know that the Lord Jesus is indeed a heavenly doctor who heals those who have a contrite heart and gives medicine to heal their sickness. People who have not had this experience must believe Jesus when he said about himself, '"The Spirit of the Lord is on me, because he has anointed me to preach good news to the poor. He has sent me to proclaim freedom for the prisoners and recovery of sight for the blind, to release the oppressed, to proclaim the year of the Lord's favour." Then he rolled up the scroll, gave it back to the attendant and sat down' (Luke 4:18–20).

If people still doubt this let them draw near to Christ themselves and experience him for themselves and learn at first hand the meaning of this incident from the gospels:

> While Jesus was having dinner at Matthew's house, many tax collectors and 'sinners' came and ate with him and his disciples. When the Pharisees saw this, they asked his disciples, 'Why does your teacher eat with tax collectors and "sinners"?' On hearing this, Jesus said, 'It is not the healthy who need a doctor, but the sick. But go and learn what this means: "I desire mercy, not sacrifice." For I have not come to call the righteous, but sinners.' (Matt. 9:10–13).

We must continue this subject.

There are some people who have become very tired with spiritual exercises, have become lukewarm and feel faint in their spirits as they walk in sadness along the ways of the Lord. What once filled them with joy now fills them with dryness and makes them tired, and they frequently grumble about their condition. They complain that their days and nights are long, and they say with Job, 'When I lie down I think, "How long before I get up?" The night drags on, and I toss till dawn' (Job 7:4).

When a soul is in this kind of state the Lord may, out of his compassion, come close to it as it travels and the One from heaven may speak heavenly things to the soul, or sing to us some delightful song from the Songs of Sion, or tell us something about the city of God, the peace of that city, the eternity of that peace or the certainty of that eternity. If the Lord does choose to do this I am certain that

the wonder of this conversation will be like a soft couch to
that tired, sleeping soul. This heavenly talk will drive
away all negative thinking from the mind and all weari-
ness from the body. Do you not think that he who wrote,
'My soul is weary with sorrow; strengthen me according
to your word' (Ps. 119:28), must have experienced this
trial and prayed for this same heavenly assistance? And
when you have received this heavenly blessing will you
not also cry out, 'Oh, how I love your law! I meditate on
it all day long' (Ps. 119:97)?

All our meditations on the Word, who is the Bridegroom, on his glory, his greatness, his power and his
grace are nothing less than words spoken by him to our
souls. This is the case, not only when he speaks, but also
when we eagerly reflect in our minds on God's judgments, when we meditate on his law night and day. Then
we shall know for certain that the Bridegroom is present
and is speaking to us in such a delightful way that we do
not become weary in our work.

There is another area in which it is not only dangerous
to be deceived, but can even prove fatal to us. We must
never attribute to ourselves the work which is in fact
being done by God in us. We must never think that God's
words speaking to our hearts are only our own thoughts.
Just as good is totally different from bad so God's words
to us and our thoughts are poles apart from each other.
Evil can never come from the Word and good can never
come from the human heart unless the Word has first
planted the seed there.

Watch out for false prophets. They come to you in
sheep's clothing, but inwardly they are ferocious
wolves. By their fruit you will recognise them. Do
people pick grapes from thornbushes, or figs from
thistles? Likewise every good tree bears good fruit, but
a bad tree bears bad fruit. A good tree cannot bear bad
fruit, and a bad tree cannot bear good fruit. Every tree
that does not bear good fruit is cut down and thrown

87

into the fire. Thus, by their fruit you will recognise them (Matt. 7:15–20).

I believe that this has been clearly stated so that it is now easy to recognise what is of God in our hearts and what comes from ourselves.

This shows to the enemies of grace that without grace in our hearts we are incapable of thinking anything good and that right thinking is a gift from God. So the soul concludes that the good things which it thinks are from God and not from its own thinking. So when you do hear God's voice speaking to you in your own heart recognise it for what it is. Take great care that the voice which comes from God's mouth does not return to him empty, but achieves the purpose for which it was sent. Then you will be able to say, 'by the grace of God I am what I am, and his grace to me was not without effect' (1 Cor. 15:10).

The soul which has the Word as its inseparable companion will be happy indeed. It will be continually delighted by its divine friend and will also be set free from its own vices because it is 'making the most of every opportunity, because the days are evil' (Eph. 5:16). This soul will not be dejected and tired out, as the Scripture says, 'No harm befalls the righteous' (Prov. 12:21).

I also think that the Lord appears to some people as the wonderful father of a family, or as a king with regal splendour. The people he appears to in this way are those who are coming close to him with a raised heart, with freedom of spirit, with a pure conscience and who are used to setting their hearts on higher spiritual things. Such souls are restless and eager to penetrate deeper mysteries, to attempt higher achievements, to attain greater perfection, not in worldly things, but in sanctification. These souls, on account of the greatness of their faith, are found to be worthy to be led into the fullness of God's presence. The God of all knowledge will never withhold himself from such strong souls, who thirst for truth and who are devoid of vanity. Such a person was Moses, who dared to ask that he might see God's glory.

And the Lord said to Moses, 'I will do the very thing you have asked, because I am pleased with you and I know you by name.' Then Moses said, 'Now show me your glory.' And the Lord said, 'I will cause all my goodness to pass in front of you, and I will proclaim my name, the Lord, in your presence. I will have mercy on whom I will have mercy, and I will have compassion on whom I will have compassion. But,' he said, 'you cannot see my face, for no-one may see me and live.' Then the Lord said, 'There is a place near me where you may stand on a rock. When my glory passes by, I will put you in a cleft in the rock and cover you with my hand until I have passed by. Then I will remove my hand and you will see my back; but my face must not be seen.' (Exod. 33:17–23).

Philip was the same kind of person. He asked that he and his fellow disciples might be shown the Father: 'Lord, show us the Father and that will be enough for us' (John 14:8).

Thomas was a similar kind of person. He refused to believe in the resurrection of Jesus unless he could touch our Lord's wounded hands and put his hand into his pierced side.

Now Thomas (called Didymus), one of the Twelve, was not with the disciples when Jesus came. So the other disciples told him, 'We have seen the Lord!' But he said to them, 'Unless I see the nail marks in his hands and put my finger where the nails were, and put my hand into his side, I will not believe it.' A week later his disciples were in the house again, and Thomas was with them. Though the doors were locked, Jesus came and stood among them and said, 'Peace be with you!' Then he said to Thomas, 'Put your finger here; see my hands. Reach out your hand and put it into my side.

Stop doubting and believe.' Thomas said to him, 'My Lord and my God!' Then Jesus told him, 'Because you have seen me, you have believed; blessed are those who have not seen and yet have believed.' (John 20:24–9)

Thomas is an example of lack of faith, but Thomas's request came from a great soul which in its own way is wonderful. In a similar way David said, 'My heart says of you, "Seek his face!"' (Ps. 27:8). Such souls aspire to great things because they are great, and because they do aspire to great things they attain them, just as God has promised them. 'Every place where you set your foot will be yours' (Deut. 11:24). Great faith deserves to be richly rewarded. You will receive good things from the Lord, depending on how much you confidently set out to attain them.

So while God spoke to other prophets in types and figures, through visions and dreams, he made himself known to Moses face to face.

When a prophet of the Lord is among you, I reveal myself to him in visions, I speak to him in dreams. But this is not true of my servant Moses; he is faithful in all my house. With him I speak face to face, clearly and not in riddles; he sees the form of the Lord' (Num. 12:6–8).

Philip was shown the Father in the Son because of his faithful prayers. To Philip's question, 'show us the Father' (John 14:8),

Jesus answered: 'Don't you know me, Philip, even after I have been among you such a long time? Anyone who has seen me has seen the Father. How can you say, 'Show us the Father'? Don't you believe that I am in the Father, and that the Father is in me? The words I say to you are not just my own. Rather, it is the Father, living in me, who is doing his work. Believe me when I say that I am in the Father and the Father is in me; or at least believe on the evidence of the miracles themselves. I tell you the truth, anyone who has faith in me will do what I have been doing. He will do even greater things than these, because I am going to the Father. And I will do whatever you ask in my name, so that the Son may bring glory to the Father. You may ask me for anything in my name, and I will do it (John 14:9–14).

Thomas was granted his wish and was allowed to touch Jesus. Jesus did not refuse the request he voiced with his lips.

And what shall I say of David? Do not the following verses indicate that his prayers must have been answered? 'I will allow no sleep to my eyes, no slumber to my eyelids, till I find a place for the Lord, a dwelling for the Mighty One of Jacob' (Ps. 132:3–4). A great Bridegroom will present himself to great souls and he will treat them in a magnificent way, sending them his light and his truth to lead them at last to his holy mountain and into his tabernacles. Those who are blessed in this way will say, 'the Mighty One has done great things for me' (Luke 1:49). 'Your eyes will see the king in his beauty' (Isa. 33:17). God will go before him leading him to the oases in the desert, where fragrant roses flower, next to the lilies of the valley, in a beautiful shaded garden with its silver fountains, storage sheds overflowing with good things, the air filled with perfumes, and last of all, the hidden precincts of the room of the king.

These are the treasures of wisdom and knowledge which are hidden in the Bridegroom which give life and are prepared to revive godly souls. Happy is the man whose longing for them has been fully satisfied! This person must be warned about one thing. He must not desire to possess exclusively gifts which would supply the needs of many other people. Maybe the reason why the Bridegroom is described as having the character of a pastor is to warn the greatly gifted person that he should share these gifts with the flock who may not be able to attain these good things through their own efforts. In the same way sheep do not like to go out looking for green pasture without their shepherd. The bride notes this carefully and this is why she wants to know where the Bridegroom feeds his flock and where he shelters from the midday sun. We must understand from this that she wishes to feed her flock with him because they are safe under his protection. The bride does not think that it is safe for the flock to stray far from the chief pastor because of the danger of being attacked by wolves, especially from the attacks of those who come dressed in sheep's clothing, but are really wolves underneath. So the bride is keen to feed in the same fields and rest in the same shade as the Bridegroom.

The bride explains her motives in this in the following words, 'Tell me, you whom I love, where you graze your flock and where you rest your sheep at midday. Why should I be like a veiled woman beside the flocks of your friends?' (S. of S. 1:7). The 'veiled woman' is a reference to those people who wish to appear to be friends of the Bridegroom but who really are not. They are only interested in feeding their own flock, not his. They are like those people who go about saying, '"Look, here is the Christ!" or, "Look, there he is!"' (Mark 13:21) so that they can lead people astray, take them from Christ's flock and add them to their own.

That is the plain meaning of the text. As far as the spiritual, hidden meaning of the text is concerned, I propose to defer its consideration for another sermon. I trust that through your prayers and in the fullness of God's mercy he will allow me to deliver this sermon, who is the Bridegroom of the Church, Jesus Christ our Lord, who is above all, God be blessed for ever. Amen.

Sermon 33

The things that a devout soul should constantly seek

'Tell me, O thou whom my soul loveth, where thou feedest, where thou makest thy flock to rest at noon: for why should I be as one that turneth aside by the flocks of thy companions?' (S. of S. 1:7 AV). Notice, first of all, how beautifully the bride distinguishes between the love of the Spirit and the love of the flesh as she wants to express more affection towards her beloved than just to say his name. She does not say 'him whom I love', but, 'O thou whom my soul loveth' and so showing the affection of her soul. Then pay particular attention to what she finds so desirable about the place where the Bridegroom pastures his flock.

Do not let it escape your attention that the bride speaks about noon and asks especially about the place where he is going to feed his flock and rest them. All this is a great sign of security. I believe that the word 'rest' was used because in that land it was unnecessary always to be standing up and awake while keeping the flock safely. For even when a shepherd is inactive and reclining under the trees his flock can walk about the fields as they please. The place where sheep can go in and out at will with nothing to make them afraid is a happy one. Who will allow me to see you, with myself, feeding on the mountains with the ninety-nine sheep which we read about in the gospel?

What do you think? If a man owns a hundred sheep, and one of them wanders away, will he not leave the ninety-nine on the hills and go to look for the one that wandered off? And if he finds it, I tell you the truth, he is happier about that one sheep than about the ninety-nine that did not wander off. In the same way your Father in heaven is not willing that any of these little ones should be lost' (Matt. 18:12–14).

The Shepherd undoubtedly rests in safety when he is next to his sheep. He does not hesitate to leave them there while he goes out to look for the one lost sheep. The bride is quite right to seek for and sigh after the place where there is food, peace, rest, security, joy and solace.

But how sad I am to be so distant from this place and I am only able to view it from afar. Every time this place is mentioned I start to cry, my heart becomes excited and I repeat the words of those who said, 'By the rivers of Babylon we sat and wept when we remembered Zion' (Ps. 137:1).

Our desire is to cry out with the bride and the Psalmist, 'Extol the Lord, O Jerusalem; praise your God, O Zion, for he strengthens the bars of your gates and blesses your people within you. He grants peace to your borders and satisfies you with the finest of wheat' (Ps. 147:12–14). Who would not want to receive peace and food and full satisfaction from this place? There is no fear or anything distasteful or any deficiency in that place. Paradise is a safe place to live in, with the Word being your delightful nourishment and all your needs amply met for all eternity.

I also have the Word on this earth, but in my human body. The Truth also feeds me through the sacrament. An angel is laden with the finest wheat and the purest grain yet it is necessary for me to be content in this life with the sacrament, and think of it as the husk. My human sinful body is like bran, the letter of the law is like chaff and faith is like a veil. These things bring with them the taste of death unless they are to some extent seasoned with the first fruits of the Spirit.

> The mind of the sinful man is death, but the mind controlled by the Spirit is life and peace; the sinful mind is hostile to God. It does not submit to God's law, nor can it do so. Those controlled by the sinful nature cannot please God. You, however, are controlled not by the sinful nature but by the Spirit, if the Spirit of God lives in you. And if anyone does not have the Spirit of Christ, he does not belong to Christ. But if Christ is in you, your body is dead because of sin, yet your spirit is alive because of righteousness. And if the Spirit of him who raised Jesus from the dead is living in you, he who raised Christ from the dead will also give life to your mortal bodies through his Spirit, who lives in you (Rom. 8:6–13).

In the same way I can only find death in the stew unless it is made harmless with some flour (see 2 Kings 4:41).

Indeed, without the Spirit even the sacrament only condemns us. 'The Spirit gives life; the flesh counts for nothing' (John 6:63). 'The letter kills, but the Spirit gives life' (2 Cor. 3:6). Without the Spirit even faith is dead.

But the Spirit breathes life into these means of grace so that I can live in them. But no matter how much the Spirit is present in these things the sacrament remains a husk, faith is only a vision and we only see God's face as if it were reflected by a dim mirror in the form of a servant.

In all these things faith is strong for me, but my understanding is weak. There is a great disparity between how I enjoy the experience of understanding and that of faith. The first is received as a result of merit and the other comes as a reward. So you can see that there is as great a difference between the nature of the nourishment as there is between the places we have referred to.

As the heavens are raised high above the earth so those who live in heaven live in a higher state with greater gifts than those who live below on earth.

Let us quickly move on, my children, to reach a safer place to live where we shall find better pasture. Let us move on quickly to a land where we can live without fear, where there is plenty of food which can be enjoyed. Lord God of Sabaoth, you judge everything but also make us safe. You are both the Lord of the armies and the Shepherd of the sheep. You provide pasture for your sheep and at the same time stay in the Sabbath rest, but that is not for us to enjoy on earth.

Until Christ's death and resurrection the whole life of Christ seemed to be like a dawn. Now the full light of his presence has transformed the dawn and the sun has risen; the morning has victoriously overtaken the night. We read in St Mark's gospel, 'Very early on the first day of the week, just after sunrise, they were on their way to the tomb' (Mark 16:2). Was it not already morning when the sun rose? But on the morning of the resurrection of Christ came a new beauty and purer and stronger light than ever before. Until then we had only known Christ from a worldly point of view 'we do so no longer' (2 Cor. 5:16).

As the Psalmist has written: 'The Lord reigns, he is robed in majesty; the Lord is robed in majesty and is armed with strength' (Ps. 93:1). Christ has now discarded the weaknesses that belonged to the flesh and is clothed in glorious robes. It is exactly the same with the sun. When it rises above the horizon it shines on the earth and warms us.

Throughout our lives Christ's presence will grow stronger. Did he not even promise, 'I am with you always, to the very end of the age' (Matt. 28:20)? But Christ does not reach the full strength of the midday sun or reveal himself in all his glory except to those to whom he chooses to reveal himself through a special vision. Lord Jesus Christ, you are the true midday sun, full of

warmth and light, banishing all shadows, drying up marshes and driving out evil diseases! You are our everlasting sun which never sets! You are our midday light in which we enjoy the freshness of spring, the beauty of summer and the deep rest and unbroken silence of winter! Or at least, if you prefer it, only the winter disappears and is missing.

The bride says, 'show me this place which is so bright, peaceful and full of God's presence.' 'Jacob called the place Peniel, saying, "It is because I saw God face to face, and yet my life was spared."' (Gen. 32:30). Moses experienced God face to face and not like other prophets through dreams and visions (see Num.12:6-8). Isaiah experienced God in the following way: 'In the year that King Uzziah died, I saw the Lord seated on a throne, high and exalted, and the train of his robe filled the temple' (Isa. 6:1). Paul relates how he experienced God,

I know a man in Christ who fourteen years ago was caught up to the third heaven. Whether it was in the body or out of the body I do not know – God knows. And I know that this man – whether in the body or apart from the body I do not know, but God knows – was caught up to paradise. He heard inexpressible things, things that man is not permitted to tell (2 Cor. 12:2–4).

'Have I not seen Jesus our Lord?' (1 Cor. 9:1) was Paul's claim. I pray that I also may become worthy to look at you, Lord Jesus, in your own light and beauty as my soul sees you feeding your flock even more abundantly and safely than you do in this life.

Here on earth you do feed your flock, but they are not perfectly satisfied. You have to stand and watch over your flock to guard them from the evils of the night and you are not allowed to sit down and quietly watch over them. Here on earth the light is poor, the food is not fully satisfying and the fields are not completely safe. So show me where you feed your flock and allow them to rest during the midday sun. You call me happy when I thirst and hunger after righteousness (see Matt. 5:6). How can this be compared with the kind of happiness the Psalmist described, 'Blessed are those you choose and bring near to live in your courts! We are filled with the good things of your house, of your holy temple.' (Ps. 65:4)? This blessing from God is reflected in the following words from the Psalmist, 'But may the righteous be glad and rejoice before God; may they be happy and joyful' (Ps. 68:3). Even if I suffer for the sake of God's righteousness I am blessed. 'If you are insulted because of the name of Christ, you are blessed, for the Spirit of glory and of God rests on you' (1 Pet. 4:14).

It is true that you are given strength and joy when you suffer, but that does not keep you safe. Having suffering and strength together is nothing other than painful joy. Everything that I experience here on earth falls short of being perfect and much of what happens is beyond prayer and it is unsafe. So when will God fill me with the joy of his presence? 'Your face, Lord, I will seek' (Ps. 27:8). Your presence is the midday sun to me. Tell me where you feed and rest your flocks at midday. I know enough about feeding but nothing about resting. Tell me where you do both of these together. I know where you do this at different times during the day, but not at midday. During my earthly pilgrimage I have become used to being spiritually fed and to feed other people with your food from the Law, the Prophets and the Psalms. You also feed us from the Gospels and I have rested in the book of the Acts of the Apostles. I have often looked for and found spiritual nourishment in the deeds and the words of the saints. Even more frequently, because it was so close at hand for me, I have eaten the bread of sorrow and the wine of remorse. 'My tears have been my food day and night, while men say to me all day long, "Where is your God?"' (Ps. 42:3). I have indeed been fed at your table, for, 'You prepare a table before me in the presence of my enemies' (Ps. 23:5). From your table I receive your gift of mercy, which comforts and consoles my sorrowful and troubled soul. I know about these pastures which I have discovered as I have followed you, my Shepherd. Now, I beg you, reveal to me the pastures I have never seen.

Sermon 36

Knowledge of literature is good for instruction, but knowledge about our spiritual weakness is more useful for our salvation

You know that today I intend to speak about ignorance, or rather different kinds of ignorance. A distinction needs to be made between two kinds of ignorance: ignorance about ourselves and ignorance about God. Both kinds of ignorance must be avoided because they both lead us to be condemned by God. First of all we must ask whether every kind of ignorance leads to condemnation. It seems to me that this is not the case. There are many things we can be ignorant of which do not put our salvation at risk. For example you may be ignorant about some complicated piece of machinery or about some industrial process without affecting your salvation.

Many people have been saved and please God in both their actions and character who are not at all familiar with the liberal arts, even though they do have their uses. How many people are mentioned in the Letter to the Hebrews as being dear to God and who know nothing about refined literature but who have a pure conscience and sincere love? (See Heb. 11.)

Many other people pleased God, not on account of the literature they knew, but by the lives they lived. Peter and Andrew, the sons of Zebedee, and all their fellow disciples, were not drawn from the school of rhetoric or philosophy and yet the Saviour used them to spread the knowledge of salvation throughout the world. They did not possess greater wisdom than other men but God saved them because of their faith and gentleness. They told the world about the way to life, not through magnificent preaching, or from clever human learning, because the world can never know God from its own wisdom.

> When I came to you, brothers, I did not come with eloquence or superior wisdom as I proclaimed to you the testimony about God. . .For Christ did not send me to baptise, but to preach the gospel – not with words of human wisdom, lest the cross of Christ be emptied of its power. . .For since in the wisdom of God the world through its wisdom did not know him, God was pleased through the foolishness of what was preached to save those who believe (1 Cor. 2:1; 1:17, 21).

It may seem to you that I speak too harshly about knowledge, as if I am blaming people for being educated and forbidding the study of literature. But I am not trying to do this at all. I am fully aware how well-read sons of the Church have served the Church as they have repulsed attacks from her enemies and have taught the uneducated. I have also read in the prophet, 'my people are destroyed from lack of knowledge. Because you have rejected knowledge, I also reject you as my priests; because you have ignored the law of your God, I also will ignore your children' (Hos. 4:6). I am also aware of what Daniel said on this subject, 'Those who are wise will shine like the brightness of the heavens, and those who lead many to righteousness, like the stars for ever and ever' (Dan. 12:3).

However, I also read that 'Knowledge puffs up' (1 Cor. 8:1), and, 'For with much wisdom comes much sorrow; the more knowledge, the more grief' (Eccles. 1:18).

There is a difference between these types of knowledge; one makes a professor wise while the other makes him vain. I will not ask you to say which is the most conducive for salvation: that which puffs up or that which brings sadness! I expect that you would choose the latter as pain can lead to health as a swelling can bring to your attention that something is wrong and action is needed. The person who seeks for salvation is close to receiving it. 'For everyone who asks receives; he who seeks finds; and to him who knocks, the door will be opened' (Luke 11:10). God loves to heal the broken-hearted, but hates people who are inflated with pride. As the wisest person has said, 'God opposes the proud but gives grace to the humble' (Jas. 4:6). The apostle Paul writes, 'For by the grace given me I say to every one of you: Do not think of yourself more highly than you ought, but rather think of yourself with sober judgment, in accordance with the measure of faith God has given you' (Rom. 12:3). God does not forbid all knowledge, only the kind of knowledge which makes you vain. What does Paul mean when he writes about 'sober' judgment? He means that you are to guard against all knowledge that does not lead to salvation and all knowledge that does not help you to progress spiritually, for we do not have much time here on earth.

All knowledge that is founded on the truth is food in itself. It is necessary for you, since there is so little time, to 'continue to work out your salvation with fear and trembling' (Phil. 2:12). You must take care, first of all, carefully to acquire what you think will help you in your salvation. Do not doctors tell you what food to eat so that different parts of your body may be cured? Although every kind of food is good in itself, since God created it, yet some food can harm you if you do not eat it properly and at the correct time. Apply what I say about food for the body to the different kinds of knowledge, since knowledge is food for the mind.

It is best that I direct you to the Master, for this teaching is not our own but comes from him; or, rather, it is ours, because it is the word of Truth. 'The man who thinks he knows something does not yet know as he ought to know' (1 Cor. 8:2). You see that a person will not praise somebody who knows many things if he himself is unable to see them. This is exactly how he views the usefulness of knowledge. What does he mean by the phrase 'the manner of knowing'? What else can he mean other than in what order, how eager we are to acquire knowledge and with what intention we ought to know all things? In what order? That is to say we should first of all acquire knowledge that will help us in our salvation. How are we to be eager? Here we are to learn that we should apply ourselves with the greatest earnestness to everything that helps us to love God with all our hearts.

What is the intention we should have in seeking to know everything? We should not seek to learn anything just so that we can pander to our pride, indulge our curiosity, but only so that we can edify ourselves and our neighbours. People should not indulge themselves in learning if they are going to be the only people to profit from what they learn. Others only learn so that they can be looked up to as learned people which is nothing short of ridiculous vanity. These people do not escape the censure of the poet and satirist Persius who wrote about such people: 'To know a thing is nothing in your eyes, unless some other person is aware of your knowledge.' Other people have making money as their motivation for acquiring learning and this is hardly a noble ideal. But there are some people who want to learn so that they can edify others and this is Christian love in action. Lastly, there are those who want to learn for their own edification which is one way of being prudent.

Sermon 38

Ignorance of God leads us to despair

What is the result of being ignorant about God? Despair
– as I have already stated. We now consider how this
occurs. Perhaps a man comes to his senses and sincerely
condemns himself for all his evil deeds. He then wants to
reform and leave his evil road and his sensual thoughts
and actions behind him.

But what if he does not know about God's goodness,
mercy, gentleness and favour towards penitent people
and how willing he is to forgive such people? Will this
man then use his sinful mind and say, 'What are you
doing? Do you want to lose out in this life as well in the
future life? Aren't your sins too great and too many? If
you could cut off the skin from your bones you could not
make recompense for your numerous offences. You have
a weak constitution and as you have lived in comfort you
will not find it easy to change the habits of a lifetime.'

This unhappy man then becomes desperate because of
these and similar arguments and so he returns to his
former evil ways. He does not realise how easy it is for the
goodness of Almighty God to break through all these obstacles for him.

After this comes a settled state of impenitence which is
the worst of all conditions to be in and which is the blasphemy which cannot be forgiven.

He who is not with me is against me, and he who does
not gather with me scatters. And so I tell you, every sin

and blasphemy will be forgiven men, but the blasphemy against the Spirit will not be forgiven. Anyone who speaks a word against the Son of Man will be forgiven, but anyone who speaks against the Holy Spirit will not be forgiven, either in this age or in the age to come (Matt. 12:30–2).

The impenitent man becomes deeply upset, is taken over by excessive sadness and such a deep melancholy that he refuses to come out of it or to be consoled in it. He is in the state about which the Scripture says: 'When wickedness comes, so does contempt, and with shame comes disgrace' (Prov. 18:3).

He may prefer to close his eyes to his miserable state and deceive himself with some kind of plausible excuse and throw himself irrevocably back into the pleasures of the world and enjoy them as much as he can. 'While people are saying, "Peace and safety", destruction will come on them suddenly, as labour pains on a pregnant woman, and they will not escape' (1 Thess. 5:3). So, from ignorance of God stems the consummation of all evil, which is despair.

The apostle Paul says that 'there are some who are ignorant of God' (1 Cor. 15:34), and I say that all those who are unwilling to be converted to God are without knowledge of God. Doubtless, they do this only because they imagine God to be unkind and severe, when in reality he is kind and good. They imagine that God is hard and implacable, when he is full of mercy; they imagine him to be cruel when he is to be loved above everyone else. They are totally deceived and put an idol in the place of God. Why are you so fearful, you people of such little faith? Do you think that Christ is unwilling to forgive you your sins? When Christ's hands were nailed to the cross he also nailed your sins to the cross.

Are you reluctant to turn away from your evil ways because you are feeble and have been brought up in the lap of luxury? Christ knows the clay that you were made from. Do you believe that you are used to evil and bound by the habit of sin like an iron chain? But remember that, 'The Lord sets prisoners free' (Ps. 146:7).

Perhaps you are afraid of God's anger because of the large number of your sins so that he will be reluctant to give you his helping hand? You can take heart from the words of the apostle Paul, 'where sin increased, grace increased all the more' (Rom. 5:20).

Are you worried and anxious about your food and clothes and other things that you need for your body and so are reluctant to give up what you own? Remember that, 'your heavenly Father knows that you need them' (Matt. 6:32).

What more could you want? What else holds you back from embracing salvation? It is exactly what I have been saying, it is your ignorance of God. You are not prepared to believe what I am telling you about him. I wish only that you would believe those who tell you about their own experience of God. If you do not believe you will never have understanding. But that faith is not given to all.

God grant that we may never suffer from this kind of ignorance about God which the Bible has warned us against. On the bride has been bestowed not only knowledge but also friendship and intimate fellowship with him who is not only her Bridegroom but also her God. Without any trace of fear, she asks him: 'Tell me, you whom I love, where you graze your flock and where you rest your sheep at midday' (S. of S. 1:7). Here the bride is not only asking to see the Bridegroom but also the place where his glory resides. In reality, this place and his glory are none other than himself. The Bridegroom reproves her for her presumption and warns her to know herself and the limits that should restrain her. The bride believes that she can receive this great vision, perhaps, because she is so caught up by her love for the Bridegroom that she forgets that she is still human and the divine brightness is inaccessible to her at present.

St Paul wrote about this:

I charge you to keep this command without spot or blame until the appearing of our Lord Jesus Christ, which God will bring about in his own time – God, the blessed and only Ruler, the King of kings and Lord of lords, who alone is immortal and who lives in unapproachable light, whom no-one has seen or can see. To him be honour and might for ever. Amen (1 Tim. 6:13–16).

The bride is immediately convicted about her ignorance and ceases to be presumptuous. 'If you do not know, leave.' This is the terrifying message of the Bridegroom to his beloved. He now speaks as her Master rather than as her Bridegroom. He is not angry, but he wants her to be made pure so that she is capable of receiving the vision she desires. For that vision is reserved for the pure in heart.

Sermon 43

How meditating on Christ's Passion enables the bride, that is, the faithful soul, to journey uninjured through the prosperity and adversity of this world

'My lover is to me a sachet of myrrh resting between my breasts' (S. of S. 1:13). Previously the Bridegroom had been called 'the king', now he is called, 'my lover'. Before he was in his royal banqueting room now he is happy to be with his bride. Humility is a great virtue since the majestic godhead himself condescends to it so readily. Reverence can quickly be transformed into friendship and the person who was distant can be brought close in a moment.

'My lover is to me a sachet of myrrh'. Myrrh, which is bitter, represents the hard facts of trouble and sorrow. The bride can see that she is about to endure these for the sake of her Beloved and so says these words with joy, trusting that she will be able to endure everything that she has to go through. In a similar way it was said of the apostles, 'The apostles left the Sanhedrin, rejoicing because they had been counted worthy of suffering disgrace for the sake of the Name' (Acts 5:41). So the bride refers to him, not as a weighty mass, but as a small bundle to show that whatever suffering comes to her she thinks that is very little for the sake of the Bridegroom's love. The bride correctly called it small and light because he was a small child when he was born. 'For to us a child is born' (Isa. 9:6). Again it is a small and light bundle. As the apostle Paul said, 'I consider that our present sufferings are not worth comparing with the glory that will be revealed to us' (Rom. 8:18). He also said, 'our light and momentary troubles are achieving for us an eternal glory that far outweighs them all' (2 Cor. 4:17). So what is now a small bundle of myrrh will one day be turned into eternal glory which makes the burden of the myrrh pale into insignificance.

Is it not a little bundle of myrrh we have to bear since his yoke is easy and his burden is light? 'Come to me, all of you who are weary and burdened, and I will give you rest. Take my yoke upon you and learn from me, for I am gentle and humble in heart, and you will find rest for your souls. For my yoke is easy and my burden is light' (Matt. 11:28–30). The burden is not light in itself because the severity of suffering and the bitterness of death are not light, but to the loving heart it seems easy to endure them. For this reason the bride does not only say: My beloved is a bundle of myrrh, but she adds the words 'to me' – that is to say, 'to me who loves him'. She also calls him 'my lover' indicating that her love has power to overcome the bitterness of all the troubles and that it is as strong as death (see S. of S. 8:6). You may be certain that she is not glorying in herself, but in the Lord, and that she is not relying on her own strength and bravery but on help from the Lord. To prove this she says, 'My lover . . . is resting between my breasts' (S. of S. 1:13). Because of this she can say in complete confidence, with the Psalmist, 'Even though I walk through the valley of the shadow of death, I will fear no evil, for you are with me; your rod and your staff, they comfort me' (Ps. 23:4).

We have to be sympathetic with others both in their joy and in their sorrow. As the apostle Paul has written, 'Rejoice with those who rejoice; mourn with those who mourn' (Rom. 12:15). The bride lives in danger from prosperity and from adversity. She wants to have her Beloved on her breast, near her heart. Then she can be strengthened by his power from both dangers. She is not

too elated in times of rejoicing and she is not too cast
down in times of sorrow. You, too, if you are wise, will
imitate the wisdom of the bride. You will never allow that
bundle of myrrh, which you hold so dear, and through
which you have fellowship with the sufferings of the Master, to be taken from you. You will always keep in your
mind the bitter pains he bore for you, and always meditate on them so that with the bride you may say, 'My lover
is to me a sachet of myrrh resting between my breasts'
(S. of S. 1:13).

From the beginning of my conversion I have always
tried to place this little bundle of myrrh for my individual
needs. I have collected all the cares and bitter experiences
of my Lord and have always kept them close to my breast.
These include, to start with, the privations of his infant
years, then, the labours he went through as he preached
and travelled everywhere, his waiting on God in prayer,
his fasts and temptations, his tears and compassion, the
traps that were set for him in discussions, and, last of all,
dangers from false brethren, insults, being spat on,
beaten, abused, scorned, pierced by nails, and other
things, which Christ suffered for the salvation of mankind. All these experiences of Christ may be collected up,
like wood, from the Gospels. Among all the branches of
fragrant myrrh you must not pass over what Christ
endured on the cross nor how he was embalmed in the
tomb. On the cross Christ dealt with the bitterness of my
sins and in the tomb he declared that my body would
enjoy immortality. As long as I live I shall proclaim aloud
the abundance of the graces which come from these
events. I shall never forget these mercies because I have
been restored to life through them.

It was about these mercies that godly David spoke with
tears, 'Let your compassion come to me that I may live'
(Ps. 119:77). Another saint had them in mind when he
said with tears, 'Great are the mercies of the Lord.' How
many kings and prophets have longed to see the things
which I see and have not seen them. They have laboured

and I have entered into their labours. I have reaped the harvest of myrrh which they had planted. This particular bundle has been reserved for me. No one shall take it from me. It shall lie between my breasts.

You become wise by meditating on these things. From this meditation comes righteousness, full knowledge, many merits and the riches of salvation. These meditations sometimes include bitter experiences and sometimes the sweet blessings of consolation. In adversities they lift me up and in prosperity they keep a check on my exuberant joy. Between the sadnesses and joys of this life they enable me to walk safely along the royal road that leads to life as I am protected from danger on both sides.

The Judge of the whole world has shown me that Jesus is both gentle and humble. Jesus is not only willing to receive me and to pardon me, but even more, he who is far above all powers has been given to me to be my model to imitate. This is why I so frequently talk about the sufferings of Jesus, as you know, and why they are always in my heart, as God knows. Jesus's sufferings are the constant theme of all my writings, as is well known. In a word, my philosophy is this, and it is the highest one in the world: to know Jesus and him crucified. 'I resolved to know nothing while I was with you except Jesus Christ and him crucified' (1 Cor. 2:2). I do not ask, as the bride does in this passage from the Song of Songs, 'Tell me . . . where do you rest your sheep at midday?' (1:7). For I embrace him with joy and happiness as he is always on my breast and in my heart. I do not ask, 'Tell me . . . where do you graze your flock?' for I look at him as my Saviour, as he hangs on the cross. The former of these is loftier than the latter, but the latter is sweeter than the former. One is bread and the other is milk. One is food for children and the other is nourishment which infants discover at their mothers' breasts. Therefore Christ will lie between my breasts.

My dearest Christian friends, you must also collect up a precious bundle and put it in the depths of your heart, strengthen the gateway to your breasts with it so that it may also stay between your breasts.

Let Jesus be borne, not behind you, or on your shoulders as a burden, but in front of you and before your eyes. If you do carry him and do not experience his sweetness you will be burdened by his weight and not refreshed by his fragrance rising up before you. Remember how Simeon took Jesus up into his arms, how Mary bore him in her womb, nursed him at her breasts, and, not to leave anything out, how Zachariah prophesied about him, as others did also. I suppose that Joseph must also have taken the baby Jesus on his knees and smiled at him and taken delight in him. All these people put Jesus in front of them and did not put him behind them. They should be your example and you should do the same as they did. You must have Jesus constantly before your eyes. Then you will clearly see the pains that the Lord endured for you and you will then willingly bear your own pains through his help. Jesus is the Bridegroom of the Church and is above all. May God be blessed for ever. Amen.

Sermon 45

How the soul speaks to God, the Word,
and how the Word speaks to the soul

'How beautiful you are, my darling! Oh, how beautiful!
Your eyes are doves' (S. of S. 1:15). For the Word to call
a soul 'beloved', and to say, 'How beautiful you are', is to
pour on it the grace which enables it to love and to know
that it is loved. In the same way, when the soul speaks of
the Word as her beloved and speaks about him being full
of beauty she is referring to the grace that she has to love
him and to be loved by him. She admires his condescension and wonders at his great love. His beauty comes as a
result of his love and his love is greater than any other
love because he was the first one to love. 'This is love: not
that we loved God, but that he loved us and sent his Son
as an atoning sacrifice for our sins' (1 John 4:10). For this
reason the bride cries from the depths of her heart and
with all the strength of her strongest affections, that she
is bound to love her beloved. She will do this even more
ardently because he first loved her.

So the speech of the Word is an infusion of grace and
the soul responds by giving thanks and glory to the Word.
The bride loves more and more ardently because she
feels that the love of her beloved surpasses her own love.
Her love is greater because her beloved's love preceded
her own. This is why the bride is not content to say just
once that her beloved is beautiful. She repeats her praise
of him, 'How beautiful you are, my darling! Oh, how
beautiful!' (S. of S. 1:15), in order to heighten her praise

113

of him through this repetition.

Another reason why this phrase is repeated may be because it refers to the two natures of Christ; in one we see the beauty of nature and in the other we see grace. How beautiful you are to your angels, O Lord Jesus, you are in the form of God, in your eternal nature, begotten before the morning star, shining with splendour in your saints, you are in the form and splendour of the Father, in whom the glory and brightness of eternal life are for ever resplendent! How august you are also to me, O my Lord, when I contemplate you in your glorious state! Even when you emptied yourself of your glory, when you set on one side the rays of splendour that correctly belong to your unfailing light, even then your kindness shone more brightly, your love was more conspicuous and your grace more radiant. O star out of Jacob, how beautiful you are to me as you rise. O branch springing out of the stem of Jesse (see Is. 11:1), how bright is your flower. O dayspring from on high, in what wonderful light you have visited me, who sat in darkness (see Luke 1:78).

Christ is the object of wonder and adoration even to the heavenly beings, in his conception by the Holy Spirit, in his birth by the virgin Mary, in his sinless life, in the flowing streams of his teaching, in the glistening brightness of his miracles and in the mysteries which are revealed in his sacraments!

Sun of righteousness, you arise in a blaze of glory from the heart of the earth, after your setting! King of glory, you return to heaven in resplendent clothes! At the sight of all these marvels I do nothing else than cry, All my bones shall say, Lord, who can be compared to you?

Sermon 47

How we should take part in the divine service

Our rule declares that nothing should take precedence over our 'Service of God'. This is the name that our father Benedict wanted to give to divine worship, which is offered daily in our oratory, thus indicating how keen he was that we should apply all our hearts to that holy work. Therefore, Christian friends, I warn and entreat you, always be taken up with the praises of God with pure hearts and earnest minds. Be earnest to present yourself at the worship of the Lord, willingly and reverently. Do not arrive in a lazy frame of mind, sleepy and yawning. Do not truncate your words or miss some out altogether. Do not chant between your teeth or through your nose, with broken or lowered voice, in a lazy and effeminate manner, but enunciate the words of the Holy Spirit with manly, earnest voices, which correspond to the dignity of the subject they are speaking about. Also you must make sure that you are concentrating your mind on what you are chanting and that you are not allowing your thoughts to wander.

I am not just thinking about idle and vain thoughts. Thinking about your duties and your work should be out of your mind during this hour. However, as you go into the choir, I am not advising you to forget what you have read in your books, or the thoughts that have come as a result of my speaking in this lecture room of the Holy Spirit. These thoughts are for your edification, but they do not edify you when you reflect on them as you are chanting. The Holy Spirit is not pleased if you allow them to intrude during this time. Through his holy inspiration we are always able to conform our wills to the divine will.

Through the grace and mercy of him who is the Bridegroom of the Church, our Lord Jesus Christ, who is above all, may God be blessed for ever. Amen.

Sermon 50

Two kinds of Christian love: feeling and action

'His banner over me is love' (S. of S. 2:4). 'He has set in order charity in me' (S. of S. 2:4 Vulgate, less exactly). There is Christian love in action, and there is Christian love in feeling. I believe that the first is an explicit commandment from God that has been given to mankind. But, as far as the second is concerned, who can claim to have it in the perfect way that is envisaged? So, one is given as an order and the other is given as a reward.

We do not, however, deny that with God's grace it is possible to start attaining the latter in this life. We may even be able to make some progress in it, but we shall never be able to complete it which will only happen in the future life. So why has something been commanded which we cannot fulfil? You may think that this command refers to charity in feeling, which I should not contest, but you must agree with me that it is impossible for anybody completely to achieve this.

Who would dare to say that he had been successful in an area where St Paul himself confesses that he had not attained? 'Brothers, I do not consider myself yet to have taken hold of it' (Phil. 3:13). Our great teacher did not conceal from us that the scope of this task was beyond us. He did, however, direct our attention to his own weak condition so that he might direct his energies to achieve righteousness, insofar as it is possible. When God commanded these things which men are not able to achieve in their own strength he did so, not to condemn men but in order to humble them. Then every mouth would be stopped and all the world would be subject to God. 'Now we know that whatever the law says, it says to those who are under the law, so that every mouth may be silenced and the whole world held accountable to God. Therefore no-one will be declared righteous in his sight by observing the law; rather, through the law we become conscious of sin' (Rom. 3:19–20).

As we receive this commandment, we know how far short we fall from carrying it out, so we cry to heaven, and our God has pity on us. On that day we will appreciate that 'when the kindness and love of God our Saviour appeared, he saved us, not because of righteous things we had done, but because of his mercy. He saved us through the washing of rebirth and renewal by the Holy Spirit' (Tit. 3:4–5).

I should say all this provided that we agree that the charity of the heart and the charity of the feelings were both commanded through a distinct law that had been imposed on us. The reason that the law appears to refer to charity in action is that when the Lord had said: 'Love your enemies', he immediately talked about applying this principle to actions, 'do good to those who hate you' (Luke 6:27). Another Scripture says, 'If your enemy is hungry, feed him; if he is thirsty, give him something to drink. In doing this, you will heap burning coals on his head' (Rom. 12:20). These precepts relate to actions, not to affections.

Listen to what the Lord himself commands about the affections which are due to him, 'If you love me, you will obey what I command' (John 14:15). We are also told here to engage in actions if we are to obey his commands. It would have been superfluous for Jesus to warn us about doing good works if Christian love consisted entirely of feelings. This is how we are to understand the commandment, 'Love your neighbour as yourself' (Matt. 22:39), although this is not explicitly stated. Is it not perfectly clear to you that in order to fulfil the command to love one's neighbour, it is enough precisely to observe what the law of nature prescribes? 'Do to no one what you would not want done to you' (Tobit 4:15 NJB). The Lord Jesus himself also commands this: 'in everything, do to others what you would have them do to you, for this sums up the Law and the Prophets' (Matt. 7:12).

I am not saying that we should be devoid of feelings of Christian love and that our heart should remain unmoved and barren and that we should only carry out acts of charity. People who are 'senseless, faithless, heartless, ruthless' (Rom. 1:31) are reckoned to be evil by the apostle Paul.

There is a number of kinds of affection: there is the affection produced by the flesh, the affection produced by the reason and the affection which is influenced by wisdom. Paul refers to the first of these when he says, 'the sinful mind is hostile to God. It does not submit to God's law, nor can it do so. Those controlled by the sinful nature cannot please God' (Rom. 8:7–8). The affection produced by the reason is good, is in harmony with the divine law and is opposed to the affection of the flesh since it seeks to conform to God's will. The affection that is produced by wisdom is not like either of the previous two types of affection because it tastes with appreciation the sweetness of the Lord, 'Taste and see that the Lord is good' (Ps. 34:8). The affection of wisdom banishes the affection of the flesh and rewards the affection of the mind. The affection of the flesh is attractive but dishonouring to God; the affection of the mind is dry, but steady and strong; the affection produced by wisdom is full of God's blessing and sweetness.

Through the second good deeds are carried out and it consists of Christian love in this sense. This is not charity from the heart and feelings which is seasoned with the salt of wisdom and greatly blessed by God, so that the soul receives an abundance of sweetness which is in God. Charity of action does not refresh the soul with delightful inner sweetness in this way, although it does strongly assist it with the love which stems from that love itself. So St John writes, 'Dear children, let us not love with words or tongue but with actions and in truth' (1 John 3:18). Do you notice how St John distinguishes between these two loves? One love is only based on our feelings while the other love is genuine, saving Christian love.

St John says that there is false love in a lying tongue, but he does not insist on the enjoyment of active wisdom. 'Let us love with actions and in truth' he says. That is to say: let us be moved to doing good deeds rather than moved by the powerful influence of the truth and by a feeling of emotional charity. 'His banner over me is love' (S. of S. 2:4). But which of these two kinds of charity is the Song of Songs referring to? Each of them is being spoken about, and the second one is mentioned before the first. For charity of action chooses for its sphere the lower part of life, while charity of thought and feeling chooses the higher part of life.

There is, for example, no doubt that when a soul thinks correctly the love of God is preferred to the love of man, heaven is preferred to earth, eternity is preferred to time and the soul is preferred to the body. Yet in practice the total opposite is frequently, if not always, preferred. Most often, we are preoccupied with the physical well-being of our neighbour and we try to help those who are ill to get better. We do more to promote peace on earth than glory in heaven. In our anxiety about earthly interests we scarcely give a passing thought to the things that belong to eternity. When we visit somebody who is ill we are so taken up with their physical well-being that we have no time for the welfare of their soul. According to the apostle Paul, 'the parts that are unpresentable are treated with special modesty' (1 Cor. 12:23). In this way we partially fulfil the words of the Lord, 'So the last will be first, and the first will be last' (Matt. 20:16).

Who doubts that when a man is in prayer he is speaking with God? And yet how often are we torn away from prayer in order to carry out some act of charity to a person who needs our attention or advice? How often does godly quiet give place to the rush of a busy life? How often do we put to one side with a good conscience some book we are reading and go off to engage in manual labour? How often we shall carry out some worldly occupation instead of going to celebrate the Holy Eucharist! What a preposterous order we carry things out, but necessity has no law. Charity in actions obeys its own laws and starts with the last things as the Father of all orders, 'When evening came, the owner of the vineyard said to his foreman, "Call the workers and pay them their wages, beginning with the last ones hired and going on to the first."' (Matt 20:8). At least this charity is kind and takes notice of people, not making distinctions between the relative values of things, but concentrating on the necessities of people.

This is not the case with sharing in feeling. This always starts with the most important things. Wisdom puts on everything the true value. So what is naturally more important receives greater attention than what is of lesser importance.

So reason does rule this charity, but it is at least taken up with Christian love. For true charity consists in seeing people who are in the most need receive priority over everyone else. True charity also makes sure that the priorities of our reason are faithfully taken over by our affections. So you must love the Lord your God with all your heart and all your soul and with all your strength and make sure you go farther in your affections than just loving love. Charity is content with this and receives divine love in all its fullness, to which that other love is only a step. As you are completely pervaded with this divine love you will definitely know that you have a knowledge of God even though you cannot know him as he is, as this is impossible for everyone.

Then you will also have a true understanding about yourself. You will realise that there is nothing in you

121

which deserves God's love, except that you belong to God and that you have poured out all the love of which you capable. I repeat, you will know yourself as you really are when through the experience of your own love and through the affection which you give to yourself, you find that there is nothing in you that deserves your love. You only deserve to be loved because of God without whom you yourself have no existence at all.

As far as your neighbour is concerned, whom you are commanded to love as yourself, you will know him as he really is so long as he does not show himself to you in any other way than you appear to yourself. He is the same as you, a member of the human race. Because you love yourself only because you love God it follows that you love other people who love God just as you love God.

As far as an enemy is concerned, he is, as it were, nothing, because he has no love for God. Therefore you cannot love him as you love yourself, as he does not love God. But you will love him so that he may learn to love God. For it is not the same thing to love someone in order that he may love God as it is to love someone because he does already love God.

Give me a person who wholeheartedly loves God above everything else, a person who loves both himself and his neighbour to the same extent that God loves each of them. Give me a person who loves his enemy like a person who may at some time in the future turn to the love of God, a person who naturally loves his human relations very tenderly, but who loves his spiritual parents, that is those who have taught him in the Christian faith, even more abundantly because of God's grace. This person's love for everything else is governed by his love for God. He despises the earth and looks up to heaven. He uses this world, but does not abuse it. On account of an inner faculty of his soul he knows how to distinguish between the things which should be chosen and loved and the things that should be just used. He makes use of transitory things for his journey through this life while he embraces with everlasting joy the things of eternity. Show me, I ask, a person who does this and I will be bold enough to declare that he is wise. He sees things as they really are and is able with truth and confidence to boast, 'his banner over me is love' (S. of S. 2:4).

But where are we to find such a person and how can he become like this? I ask this question with tears in my eyes: how long shall we see this fragrance without tasting it? How long do we have to look forward for our distant heavenly home, without attaining it? O Truth, you are the fatherland of exiled souls and also the end of their exile! I cry out to you but am unable to enter into your kingdom. I am kept as a human being with my defiling sins and so am not worthy to be admitted. O Wisdom, your powerful guidance extends from the beginning to the end of things which you both establish and control. You dispose everything with admirable gentleness. You order, bless and bring joy to all affections, you direct actions as is necessary for our earthly needs and dispose your affections as your eternal truth demands. So we are all able to glory in you and say, 'his banner over me is love'. For you are the power of God, the wisdom of God, Jesus Christ our Lord, the Bridegroom of the Church, God above all, who is to be blessed for ever. Amen.

The endurance of the martyrs whose strength comes from Christ

'Arise, come, my darling; my beautiful one, come with me' (S. of S. 2:13). The Church does not flinch at the burning marks of the Saviour's passion, or run away from the discoloured marks of his wounds. The Church even takes delight in them and wishes that her own death may be like these. The reason why the Bridegroom says to the bride, 'My dove in the clefts of the rock, in the hiding-places on the mountainside, show me your face, let me hear your voice; for your voice is sweet, and your face is lovely' (S. of S. 2:14) is because she dedicated herself with single-minded devotion to the wounds of Christ and continually meditates on them. This is where the endurance which does not shrink from martyrdom comes from. This is the complete confidence that she has in the most high God. The martyr has nothing to fear if he can lift his eyes to that discoloured and bloodless face. He is healed by its paleness and is strengthened to become like his Master as he faced death, even to being as pale as gold. Why should we be fearful of the person who said, 'show me your face'? Why does he say this? I do not think it is so much that the Bridegroom desires to see the bride as that he desires to be seen by her. For what exists that he does not see? He has no need that anyone should show themselves to him as he sees everything, even the hidden things. So what he wants is to be seen. The leader is full of kindness and wants his devoted soldiers to fix their eyes on his wounds so that they can draw strength from them. Then these soldiers will derive power from Christ's example.

The truth of the matter is that the martyr will not feel his own pain if he is gazing at the wounds of his Saviour. He stands intrepid and triumphant, even though his body is a mass of wounds. When the sword cuts into his body and he sees the sacred blood of martyrdom pour from his body he is not only brave but happy. Where, then, is the soul of the martyr? It is in the place of safety, in the rock, in the heart of Jesus, and the soul enters in there through the open door of Christ's wounds. If the soldier was left alone with his own sensations he would certainly feel the pain and see the lunges of the sword. The pain would be impossible to endure and he would give up and deny his Lord. But because the soul is abiding in the rock it is little wonder that he endures as a rock endures.

If the soul is away from the body it is hardly surprising that it does not feel the pains of the body. This does not happen because the person is unable to feel anything, but because of the power of love. The senses are not lost they are just under control. The pain is felt but the soul rises above the pain and despises it. From this rock the martyr gains his endurance and has the power to drink from the Lord's cup. '"You don't know what you are asking," Jesus said to them. "Can you drink the cup I am going to drink?" "We can," they answered. Jesus said to them, "You will indeed drink from my cup, but to sit at my right or left is not for me to grant. These places belong to those for whom they have been prepared by my Father"' (Matt. 20:22–3). And that cup of suffering, so exciting in its passionate glow, is good indeed. 'You prepare a table before me in the presence of my enemies. You anoint my head with oil; my cup overflows' (Ps. 23:5). This cup also overflows for the leader who is keenly watching the struggle as the soldier fights and conquers because the joy of the Lord was his strength (see Neh. 8:10).

The voice of the martyr's witness which endures to the end causes the leader great joy. It is impossible that it should be otherwise. The Bridegroom earnestly asks for this in the words that are before us, 'let me hear your voice'. The Bridegroom will not be slow to reward this in line with his promise, 'Whoever acknowledges me before men, I will also acknowledge him before my Father in heaven' (Matt. 10:32).

How the Father and the Word come to the soul and the close fellowship that exists between God and the soul

The humility of the Word is so great, the generosity of the Father and the Word to the well behaved soul is so great that they deign to honour it with their presence. They do this in such a complete way that they live in the soul when they come to it. 'If anyone loves me, he will obey my teaching. My Father will love him, and we will come to him and make our home with him' (John 14:23). It is not enough that they come to the soul, they must bestow the fullness of their presence on the soul. What does it involve for the Word to come to the soul? This happens when the soul is taught wisdom. And how does the Father come to the soul? This happens when the Father touches the soul with the love of wisdom, so that it is able to say, 'I fell in love with her beauty' (Wisd. 8:2 NJB).

The Lord Jesus may deign to come to me, or rather be in me, not in anger, but in love and in a spirit of kindness. If he does come in me he will give me a godly jealousy since nothing comes more strongly from God than love. This is indeed God. This is the way in which I shall know if the Lord Jesus has come into me. He will not come alone, as the Father will come with him. For what can be more like the Father than this? This is why he is not only called the Father of the Word, but also 'the Father of compassion' (2 Cor. 1:3). It is his nature always to be compassionate and spare us. I am certain that the Bridegroom is with me whenever my mind is opened so that I can understand the Scriptures. 'Then he opened their minds so they could understand the Scriptures' (Luke 24:45). I know that this has happened when I understand the Scriptures so that I can preach about heavenly wisdom from the depths of my heart. I know that the Scriptures have been opened to my mind when I am given deeper insight into divine mysteries from God's heavenly wisdom, or when the heavens themselves seem to spread over my soul and flood it with fruitful mediations. These are the rich gifts that come to us from the Word. We receive these precious things from his abundant love.

I do not doubt that the Father is with me when I am overwhelmed by feelings of humble devotion which inspire my soul. When love of the truth so penetrates my soul that I despise my vanity and do not become proud when I acquire more knowledge, and am not exalted after a special blessing from God, then I also know that the divine fatherly hand is over me. When I persevere, as much as I am able, in the right thoughts and actions worthy of God's great humility, and know that God's grace has not been given to me in vain, then I am certain that the Father and the Word have taken up residence in me. The Father feeds my soul while the Word instructs it.

There is a close intimate relationship between the divine Word and the soul as a result of this grace and you can easily imagine the delight which flows from this close fellowship. I believe that a soul which is in this state can say, 'My beloved is mine'. The bride is aware that she loves God truly, even vehemently, and therefore concludes that she is loved by God in the same way. This soul makes every effort to please God with single-minded devotion and diligence and can therefore recall the Lord's promise, 'with the measure you use, it will be measured to you' (Matt. 7:2).

It is true that the bride is deeply thankful for the grace that has been given to her because she knows that her beloved is responsible for this gift. This is why she puts his name before hers and says, 'My lover is mine and I am his' (S. of S. 2:16). From God's attributes the bride correctly concludes that she is loved by the one she loves. This is, in fact, the case. The love of God for the soul produces the love of the soul for God. God's care for the soul produces a similar kind of care in the soul for God. When a soul starts to look at the revealed glory of the Lord it has to become transformed by God. God will then show himself to you as you have shown yourself to him. As the Psalmist says, 'To the faithful you show yourself faithful, to the blameless you show yourself blameless, to the pure you show yourself pure' (Ps. 18:25–6). So why is not God loving with the loving, attentive to the attentive and cautious with the cautious?

Lastly, the Lord says, 'I love those who love me, and those who seek me find me' (Prov. 8:17). God assures you of his love if you love him. God also promises to care for you if you keep your relationship strong with him. Are you keeping vigil? Then God will keep vigil, too.

Even if you get up in the middle of the night you will discover that God is already awake, looking out for your arrival. You will be wrong ever to think that you can be one step ahead of God. Souls which are deeply assured of these wonderful truths wonder at the thought that this majestic God can give them so much attention as if God had nobody else to look after.

I want to add just one thing, which although it appears to be incredible is, in fact, true. I direct this especially to those who are spiritually minded among you. A soul which looks at God does so in the same way that God looks at him, as if it was the only soul that God looked at. So the soul gives its full attention to God because God has given his full attention to it. How good you are, O Lord, to the soul which seeks you! You come to it, you embrace it, you reveal yourself as its Bridegroom and its husband. You are its Lord, are above everything and blessed by God for ever. Amen.

The seven things which the soul needs, which make it seek the Word. Once the soul has reformed it comes close to contemplate Christ and to enjoy the sweetness of his presence

'All night long on my bed I looked for the one my heart loves' (S. of S. 3:1). 'The soul seeks the Word and accepts his correction with joy so that she may be enlightened and receive knowledge from him. Through the help of the Word the soul attains virtue and is reformed according to his wisdom. Then she can be transformed into his likeness and the Word proceeds to make her fruitful in good deeds. Finally the soul is delighted to enjoy his presence. For all these reasons the soul seeks the Word . . .'

And now listen to the reasons for what I have said. First, notice how the soul is content to receive divine correction. We read that the Word speaks about this in the Gospels, 'Settle matters quickly with your adversary who is taking you to court. Do it while you are still with him on the way, or he may hand you over to the judge, and the judge may hand you over to the officer, and you may be thrown into prison' (Matt. 5:25).

Nothing could be more sensible. If I am not mistaken, the Word solemnly declares that he is our enemy because he opposes our sinful, human desires, as is clear when he said, 'They are a people whose hearts go astray' (Ps. 95:10).

Your reaction to this should be to run away from the impending wrath of God. But you need to know how you can make peace with your enemy. This is totally impossible if you do not agree that you are in the wrong and become an enemy to yourself. You must wage war against yourself in a continuous struggle. In short, you must renounce your evil habits and ingrained desires. This is a really hard fight. If you attempt to take this on in your own strength it will be like trying to stop a river in full flood with one finger, or like trying to make the River Jordan flow backwards. So what can you do? You must seek the Word through whose grace you can be enabled to carry out his will. Run to him for help. He opposes the evil that is in you, but through his help you may be transformed so that he will oppose you no longer. His opposition towards you will be changed into approval of you. Then the grace which he gives you will be more effective in transforming you than the most violent anger.

This is, I think, the first way in which the soul seeks the Word. If you do not know what he really desires, even though you have given yourself over to him then you may be zealous for God, but this zeal is not based on knowledge. '. . . they are zealous for God, but their zeal is not based on knowledge' (Rom. 10:2). You must not think that this ignorance can be lightly dismissed. 'If he ignores this, he himself is ignored' (1 Cor. 14:38). In this position, the first thing that you should do is to go to the Word and he will teach you his ways. Otherwise, even though you may want to do good you will not know how to and you will just wander off the right road and end up in the desert. The Word is light, as the Psalmist has said, 'The unfolding of your words gives light; it gives understanding to the simple' (Ps. 119.130). You will be happy if you can also say, 'Your word is a lamp to my feet and a light for my path' (Ps. 119.105). You will have greatly benefited if your will is changed and your reason enlightened so that you are able to desire what is good and to recognise it when it appears in you. The first gift brings life to

131

your soul and the second gift brings sight. For when the soul wanted to do evil it was dead and when it could not recognise good it was blind.

Your soul is alive, has sight and is rooted in goodness all because of the help and through the work of the Word. If the soul can stand upright it is as a result of being raised up by the hand of the Word who places it, as it were, on the two feet of devotion and understanding. Although it does stand upright it must remember, 'if you think you are standing firm, be careful that you don't fall!' (1 Cor. 10:12). Do you think that the soul which could not even stand on its own two feet can remain standing by its own strength?

I am sure that this is indeed not the case! As it was by the Word of the Lord that the heavens were made can an earthly, created being stand without him? If he could stand by himself why should a man who has been created out of the earth pray, 'strengthen me according to your word' (Ps. 119:28)? He had even experienced the inability to stand by himself, since he says, 'I was pushed back and about to fall, but the Lord helped me' (Ps. 118:13).

Does anybody ask what it was that pushed him? It was not just one person: it was the devil, it was the world, it was, perhaps, some person. You ask: what person? The truth is that every person tempts himself. Do not wonder at this. You need not worry about other people tempting you because you should be busy stopping yourself being your own tempter. As the apostle Peter has written: 'Who is going to harm you if you are eager to do good' (1 Pet. 3:13)?

So you are threatened by three enemies. The devil seeks to spread evil through his malice, the world through pride, while man stays burdened under the weight of his own corruption. The devil wants to make you evil but does not have the power to defeat you so long as you do not give in to his wicked suggestions. So we read, 'Resist the devil, and he will flee from you' (Jas. 4:7). It was the devil, because of his jealousy, who tempted and

132

overthrew those who were upright in paradise, since they did not resist him, but gave way to his own evil suggestions. Through his own pride the devil threw himself down from the height of heaven without anybody else being responsible. So you must be warned that mankind is in a very serious condition and is liable to fall because of the weight which burdens his own nature.

The world also brings evil because 'the whole world is under the control of the evil one' (1 John 5:19). Everybody feels its influence, but only those who consent to go along with it in their minds and wills are overthrown by the world. I do not want to be a friend of the world in case I fall. Anybody who seeks to be a friend of the world is God's enemy and this is the most disastrous step anyone can make. From this it seems clear that the main reason for man's downfall is himself. He can fall without anybody else being involved. But he does not have to fall if he does not want to, no matter how many other people may oppose him.

Which of these three enemies should be resisted? Clearly, we must resist the most persistent enemy. This enemy is on closer terms with us, which is enough reason in itself to make us fall. Without this closeness no enemy can make us fall. The wise man had good reason to say, 'Better a patient man than a warrior, a man who controls his temper than one who takes a city' (Prov. 16:32).

This is a very important matter for you. You are in need of great strength and this can be given to you from heaven. If you possess this strength completely you will be able to be victorious in your own soul and invincible to all other enemies. A spiritual strength has the ability to stand firm and unshakeable on the side of the right. For spiritual strength is able to direct everything according to the reason.

Who is able to climb the hill of the Lord? Who will take upon himself to climb to the top of the mountain, that is to say, to be completely virtuous? Whoever does this must bear in mind how arduous the climb is and how easy it is to fall without the help of the Word.

Happy is the soul which stirs up the joy of the angels when they look at it. The angels will then say in the soul's hearing, 'Who is this coming up from the desert leaning on her lover' (S. of S. 8:5)? All the bride's efforts are in vain if she does not lean on God. When the bride does trust in God she will acquire new resources in herself, become stronger, and be able to subordinate everything to reason. She will be able to control anger, fear and joy, like a skilful charioteer (if I am allowed to use such an analogy) as she drives the chariot of the soul. She will be able to control all her sinful, human desires and subject all her senses to the control of her reason. How can this all fail to take place in the person who is depending completely on God for everything that he does? We can be sure of being really strong if we can echo the words of the apostle Paul, 'I can do everything through him who gives me strength' (Phil. 4:13). The power of the Word is supremely seen in the power that he gives to those people who put their trust in him. Jesus said, 'Everything is possible for him who believes' (Mark 9:23). So the soul that does not rely on its own strength, but only on the strength of the Word, can master its own self and never allow unrighteousness to rule there. This is why I say that the soul which is relying on the Word and which is empowered from heaven can never be defeated or trapped by flagrant violence, secret guile or enticing temptations.

Next, we move on to consider my assertion that it is by the Word that we are reformed according to wisdom. The Word is wisdom as well as strength. So the soul must draw wisdom from the God of Wisdom and strength from the God of Strength. Both of these gifts should be credited to the Word alone. If either of them is credited to some other source, or arrogated to the soul itself, we might as well say that a river does not flow from a spring and juice does not come from a grape and that light does not come from the sun. This is a true saying, 'If any of you lacks wisdom, he should ask God, who gives generously to all without finding fault, and it will be given to him' (Jas. 1:5). What the apostle James states to be the case about wisdom is also true about strength. It is a gift from God which comes down from him who is the Father of the Word and is to be ranked among the best of gifts.

If anybody should say that this gift is in all respects identical with wisdom I shall not quarrel with him. But this becomes completely true in the Word and not in the soul. What is totally united in the Word, because of his divine nature, cannot be completely united in the soul. In the soul they are split up and used as they are needed. If this is a correct principle, it is one thing for the soul to be made strong, but another thing for it to be directed by wisdom. It is one thing for it to be strengthened by power and it is another thing for it to be delighted by sweetness.

Although wisdom is powerful and power is sweet, we must attach to each word its correct significance. We think of power as giving a certain strength to the soul. We think of wisdom giving calm and composure and a kind of spiritual sweetness to the soul. This is what I think the apostle Paul had in mind, when, after he had given many commands about spiritual strength, he mentioned the sweetness of the Holy Spirit (see 2 Cor. 6:6). We then see it as an honour to stand firm, to resist, to repel force with force, as we think that this is the fruit of strength and courage and hard work. For it is one thing to defend your honour with effort when in danger, and another thing to defend your honour and hold on to your own peace of mind. Whatever power may be carefully prepared wisdom can make use of and enjoy. What wisdom orders and contemplates strength puts into practice.

'Leisure is what gives the scribe the chance to acquire wisdom' (Ecclus. 38:25 NJB). So the very leisure of wisdom is a labour and the more leisurely wisdom is the more laborious it is in its own way. But the more virtue is exercised in its own sphere of action the more illustrious it becomes. The more virtue wins over difficulties the more approval it receives. If anyone wants to define wisdom as

135

being the love of virtue I should think him close to the truth. Wherever there is love, then any task, no matter how laborious it is, can become a pleasure and a joy.

Neither should I object if anyone defined wisdom as the love of and the taste of good. But we have nearly lost this taste from the face of the earth. As soon as mankind could reason the poison of the old serpent corrupted the palate of their heart. No longer do people have a taste for what is good since a depraved taste has taken its place. But wisdom constantly wins over wickedness in the souls it has entered into, replacing any taste for evil which wickedness has introduced. When wisdom enters a soul it cuts off its appetite for evil desires, purifies the understanding and heals and restores the palate of the heart. Once its powers have been transformed in this way it starts to seek after good things and to desire wisdom itself. There is nothing better in the whole world to do than that.

How many good actions are not motivated by joy? People who live like that do these good deeds out of necessity rather than because they have a taste for them and love to do them. And how many people engage in wrong actions, not through evil motives, but just because they are forced into them through fear or because of the want to satisfy some desire. People who deliberately do good are either wise or take delight in goodness for its own sake. People who deliberately indulge in evil do so because they have an evil disposition. Happy is the soul that only delights in good and hates evil! This is the way to be reformed and to become wise. This the way wisdom gains victory in your life. The best way for wisdom to gain victory over wickedness is when all delight in evil is banished from a soul and when the soul feels that it is whole-heartedly delighting in what is good. Then we have to look to power for enduring trials and we have to look to wisdom for the ability to delight in them. The role of power in your life is to strengthen your heart and to wait patiently for the Lord. The role of wisdom in your life is for you to taste and see how good the Lord is.

We have seen how once the will changes from evil to good the soul is restored to life, spiritual health is given by God's teaching, stability comes as the gift of strength and maturity is the result of wisdom. We have only one more gift to seek and that is the gift of beauty. Without beauty it is impossible to please Christ who is the fairest among the sons of men. For the bride is aware of the words, 'The king is enthralled by your beauty' (Ps. 45:11). How many good gifts, gifts from the Word, has the soul received? We have mentioned many: knowledge, goodwill, power and wisdom. Yet we do not read that any of these are sought for by the Word. Only 'your beauty' is mentioned. How can the Bridegroom not wish that his bride should wear the same kind of clothes as he does? The closer the bride resembles the Bridegroom the dearer she becomes.

So of what does this beauty of the soul consist? It consists in her being called honourable. Honour shows itself in outward behaviour, not that it consists in that, but it is recognised through it. Its origin and the place it lives in is the conscience. The witness of a good conscience is its glory. No brighter light ever shines than when the truth beams out of a soul and the soul sees that it is in the truth. How is this seen? It is seen when a soul is chaste, modest, self-restrained, circumspect and when it allows nothing to hinder this glory from being seen. This is further seen when the soul is not conscious of any evil deeds in its life which would make it ashamed in the presence of the truth and cause it to hide its face as if it was trying to avoid the divine light. This is undoubtedly the beauty which God takes most pleasure in seeing in the godly soul. We give this the name honour.

When the splendour of this beauty is diffused throughout the heart it has to become visible on the outside and cannot be hidden, but becomes like a light shining in a dark place which cannot be concealed. It shines its bright rays throughout the body, making it an image of the soul, and diffuses itself through every action the body makes.

137

So every action, good word, look, movement, laugh (if this person should ever laugh), is shot through with self-restraint as a result of the powerful effects of these rays. The fairness of the soul is seen when all the movements of the body are given over to righteousness, so long as no secret guile lurks there to obscure it. For it is possible to pretend that these things exist when they do not naturally come from the heart. We shall now show you this spiritual beauty in all its magnificence. It consists of a soul which is keen to unite to the witness of a good conscience within with a pure reputation outside. Or, as the apostle Paul has written, 'we are taking pains to do what is right, not only in the eyes of the Lord but also in the eyes of men' (2 Cor. 8:21). Happy is the soul that has dressed itself in the beauty of that holiness, that innocent purity, through which it may claim to be different from the world, but similar to the Word. We read about this where we are told, 'She is a reflection of the eternal light' (Wisd. 7:26 NJB), and, 'The Son is the radiance of God's glory and the exact representation of his being' (Heb. 1:3).

The soul which is in this condition ventures to think about union with the Word. Why should she not do this, as she sees that the more she becomes like him the more she is suited to spiritual marriage. The height of his majesty does not terrify her because she looks like him, her affection unites her to him, her obedience and loyalty constitute a promise to become married. This is what she says: 'I have taken an oath and confirmed it, that I will follow your righteous laws' (Ps. 119:106). The apostles did the same when they said, 'We have left everything to follow you!' (Matt. 19:27). Paul made a similar statement about human marriage which nevertheless signifies the spiritual union between Christ and his Church. 'For this reason a man will leave his father and mother and be united to his wife, and the two will become one flesh' (Eph. 5:31). In the Psalms the bride talks about herself in these terms, 'But as for me, it is good to be near God. I have made the Sovereign Lord my refuge' (Ps. 73:28).

You can tell that a soul is married to the Word and that she is his bride when you see it leave everything and cling to the Word in everything it says and does, when it lives only for the Word, when it is totally controlled by the Word, when it bears fruit because of the Word and when it can say with sincerity, 'For to me, to live is Christ and to die is gain' (Phil. 1:21).

Someone listening to me may ask: what does it mean to enjoy the Word? I think that this question should be answered by the person who has experienced this happiness. Even if I were to be given this great blessing how could I put into words and explain such a mystery? This is how one person who has had the experience described it: 'If we are out of our mind, it is for the sake of God; if we are in our right mind, it is for you' (2 Cor. 5:13). So it is one thing for me to have communion with God, and he alone is the judge of this, but it is quite another for me to talk about it with you, my Christian friends. I have been allowed to experience this great blessing, but I am not permitted to put it into words.

If you are keen to know what it is to enjoy the Word you must prepare your heart and not your ear. The tongue cannot reveal it to you, only grace can teach you about it. It is hidden from the wise and the prudent and it is revealed to babies. Humility, my Christian friends, is the great and high virtue through which you can receive what is promised, but what cannot be taught. Through humility you can attain what is impossible to be transmitted to you through teaching. Humility can enable you to become fit to receive the Word and as you receive the Word you will be receiving what words are incapable of expressing. Why is this? It is not because the soul deserves this but because it is the will of him who is the Father of the Word, the Bridegroom of the soul, Jesus Christ our Lord, who is above all. God be blessed for ever. Amen.

The Hodder and Stoughton Christian Classics Series

The Hodder and Stoughton Christian Classics are original translations, adaptations or abridgements of the great classics of devotional spirituality. Chosen for their reference to the needs of today's Christians, for their theological and spiritual perception and for the timelessness of their message, each of the titles in the series will enrich the faith of the reader.

The Confessions of St Augustine
Saint Augustine (Trans. E.M. Blaiklock)
St. Augustine's classic testimony to the grace of God.

The Cloud of Unknowing
Edited by Halcyon Backhouse
An anonymous fourteenth-century mystic's experience of knowing and serving God.

The Little Flowers of St Francis
E.M. Blaiklock and A.C. Keyes (Translated and edited by)
An inspiring and unique collection of St. Francis' sayings, stories and teaching.

Pilgrim's Progress
John Bunyan
The spiritual pilgrimage of Christian: the full version in modern English.

The Institutes of Christian Religion
John Calvin (Editors: Tony Lane, Hilary Osborne)
The most important single book of the Protestant Reformation (abridged).

The City Without a Church
Henry Drummond
Classical meditations on practical Christian living.

THE TWELVE STEPS OF HUMILITY AND PRIDE/ON LOVING GOD

Bernard of Clairvaux

These two short classics of medieval monastic spirituality by Bernard of Clairvaux, the great Cistercian monk born in 1090, are published together in a modern translation. They provide a unique insight into the mind and spirituality of Bernard, who in many ways appears surprisingly modern in his understanding of human frailty and aspirations.

On Loving God is peppered with biblical quotations and wisdom interwoven with the author's perception of his relationship with God. It is a work of deep spiritual reflection on man's response to God's love.

The Twelve Steps of Humility and Pride describes the many pitfalls and encouragements in man's search for truth, as he journeys on a spiritual 'ladder' – ascending in humility, descending in pride.